Scripture Discussion Commentary 7

SCRIPTURE DISCUSSION COMMENTARY 7

Series editor: Laurence Bright

Mark and Matthew

Mark *Sean Freyne*

Matthew *Henry Wansbrough*

ACTA Foundation
Adult Catechetical Teaching Aids
Chicago, Illinois

First published 1971

ACTA Foundation (Adult Catechetical Teaching Aids), 4848 N. Clark Street
Chicago, Illinois 60640

© 1971 Sean Freyne, Henry Wansbrough

2544

Library of Congress number 71–173033

ISBN 0 87946 006 7

Made and printed in Great Britain by
William Clowes & Sons, Limited
London, Beccles and Colchester

Contents

Contents

General Introduction

A few of the individual units which make up this series of biblical commentaries have already proved their worth issued as separate booklets. Together with many others they are now grouped together in a set of twelve volumes covering almost all the books of the old and new testaments—a few have been omitted as unsuitable to the general purpose of the series.

That purpose is primarily to promote discussion. This is how these commentaries differ from the others that exist. They do not cover all that could be said about the biblical text, but concentrate on the features most likely to get lively conversation going—those, for instance, with special relevance for later developments of thought, or for life in the church and world of today. For this reason passages of narrative are punctuated by sets of questions designed to get a group talking, though the text of scripture, helped by the remarks of the commentator, should have already done just that.

For the text is what matters. Individuals getting ready for a meeting, the group itself as it meets, should always have the bible centrally present, and use the commentary only as a tool. The bibliographies will help those wishing to dig deeper.

What kinds of group can expect to work in this way?

Absolutely any. The bible has the reputation of being difficult, and in some respects it is, but practice quickly clears up a lot of initial obstacles. So parish groups of any kind can and should be working on it. The groups needn't necessarily already exist, it is enough to have a few like-minded friends and to care sufficiently about finding out what the bible means. Nor need they be very large; one family could be quite enough. High schools (particularly in the senior year), colleges and universities are also obvious places for groups to form. If possible they should everywhere be ecumenical in composition: though all the authors are Roman catholics, there is nothing sectarian in their approach.

In each volume there are two to four or occasionally more studies of related biblical books. Each one is self-contained; it is neither necessary nor desirable to start at the beginning and plough steadily through. Take up, each time, what most interests you—there is very little in scripture that is actually dull! Since the commentaries are by different authors, you will discover differences of outlook, in itself a matter for discussion. Above all, remember that getting the right general approach to reading the bible is more important than answering any particular question about the text—and that this approach only comes with practice.

LAURENCE BRIGHT

Mark

Sean Freyne

Introduction

1. The gospel as good news

Until quite recently the tendency has been to regard the four written gospels as truncated biographies of Jesus, which when conflated with one another give a detailed account of his life and ministry as it actually was. This version of what constitutes a gospel scarcely does justice to the writers or their intentions, however. It is clear that the evangelists never thought of writing a biography of Jesus in a modern sense, nor did they feel the need to do so. Their primary concern was to ensure that those who read their works would come to a proper understanding of the meaning that Jesus as the crucified and risen one should have for their lives.

The great truth that underlies all the new testament writings is that Jesus is risen and, as promised, is present with his community, making the same demands for a change of heart as he did during his earthly life, and proclaiming the same message of love and reconciliation to those who are ready to listen. These demands and this offer are even more real now seeing that Jesus has shown in his own life the implications of his message and has been crowned with glory and honour by the Father. Everything he said and did while he was with them is seen in the light of this glorious ending, and the full meaning of his life is now disclosed for the first time, even for those who had followed him from the start. It is this meaning, illuminated by the light of the Easter experience, that the gospels have captured for us.

In a very basic sense there is only one gospel, but different circumstances and backgrounds gave rise to various problems for those who listened to the good news about Jesus. Converts from judaism had to cope with very different problems to those of gentile christians, many of whom were the outcasts of society in the larger cities of the Roman empire. It is not really surprising therefore that we have four different versions of the one gospel, each coming from different religious and social backgrounds and each addressed to different church situations. They all agree on the essential that Jesus who died in love for man has been raised by the Father, but each selects and adapts his words and his deeds to explain the meaning of faith for the particular set of readers. It is this living church situation behind each gospel that makes them such vital documents for us today. When we examine them from this point of view we will discover that many of our own personal and church problems are closely related to theirs, and that we too must come to an understanding of the gospel message within a similar situation. As we strive to recapture the gospel message in this age of renewal our study of the gospels should confront us with the person of the risen Christ, judging and saving us with the offer of real possibilities for discovering life with God as he has discovered it. They are not, and were never intended to be, mere accounts of an exemplary life of a past historical figure, no matter how inspiring in itself such a life may have been.

2. Mark's gospel: some preliminary considerations

A preliminary look at Mark's gospel reveals some interesting data which should assist us in understanding its message. By comparison with the other two synoptic gospels, Matthew and Luke, it is a relatively short document. Matthew has 1,068 verses and Luke 1,149, whereas Mark has 661, only 30 of which are special to himself. On closer examination it will be found that Mark differs from the others in form as well as length. For the most part we get very little prolonged instruction from Jesus in this gospel, a striking contrast with Matthew in particular, where a number of great discourses dominate. Several times Mark tells us that Jesus taught or that people were in admiration at his teaching, but rarely does the evangelist allow us to sample this for ourselves, with the notable exceptions of chapters 4 (parables) and 13 (discourse on the return of the Son of Man). This means that there is dramatic movement about Mark's narrative. We are confronted with a set of pictures all linked together by summaries that carry the action further and constantly challenge us to a deeper appreciation of the events being narrated.

Mark's style and manner of expression corresponds with this general impression of his work. His style is simple and his expression direct, even blunt at times, but always vivid and alive. He does not hesitate to attribute human emotions and feelings to Jesus: he is weary and falls asleep (4:38); in face of suffering he is moved to the depths of his soul with compassion (1:41); he shows anger and indignation (3:5; 10:14); he can be amazed at the turn of events (6:6) or sorrowful (3:5). Mark has an eye for the detail that brings a description to life: Jesus is asleep on a cushion (4:37); the demoniac

from the Gerasenes was shrieking and cutting himself
with stones (5:5); during the first feeding miracle the
people sat down in rows of fifty and a hundred (6:40).
Such simplicity and vividness has led some commentators to regard Mark's gospel as a straightforward, un-
theological presentation of certain facts about Jesus.
However, more recent studies have shown that one
should not be deceived by such simplicity. Mark's is a
highly sophisticated, theological viewpoint with a message of abiding importance for christians of every age.

In trying to isolate this viewpoint and determine the
evangelist's intentions more accurately some considerations of the overall structure of his work seems called for.
The order that Mark places on the material from the oral
tradition which he uses is indicative of his overall purpose and intention. The very opening verse is an announcement of the direction of the whole work. It is
about Jesus Christ, the Son of God. There are two titles
mentioned here for Jesus 'the Christ' and 'the Son of
God' and at significant stages of the gospel we shall find
these on men's lips. Peter confesses Jesus as the Christ
(8:29) and a Roman centurion confesses him as the Son
of God at the foot of the cross (15:39). These two confessions indicate stages of development in Mark's presentation. For him believing in the gospel (1:15) is
acceptance of Jesus as Son of God. This is no easy matter,
however, since Jesus' sonship is something that will only
emerge through his living out this vocation to the full.
Mark then presents the ministry of Jesus in two stages
that can be clearly distinguished from one another by
their tone and atmosphere, with the break coming at
8:29. The first stage is marked by Jesus' adopting a
chiding attitude towards disciples who should recognise
him from the actions he is performing and which event-

ually lead to a partial confession of faith by Peter. The second stage has a very different atmosphere as all is now concentrated on the suffering role that Jesus must adopt. No longer does he seek to chide his disciples into recognition but rather he strives to lead them to a deeper level of relationship with him by inviting them to participate in his fate as the only way to achieve life.

In presenting the ministry of Jesus in this way Mark may well have had in mind the sacrifice of Isaac which had undergone an amount of elaboration in late Jewish writing, and was an obvious old testament scripture for the early church to turn to in explaining positively the 'scandalous' death of Jesus. Several new testament passages such as Rom 8:32; Acts 3:25; Heb 11:17–19, have clear echoes of Isaac and his sacrifice as the story is told in Gen 22. It is the word *agapētos,* 'well beloved' which Mark uses three times for Jesus (1:11; 9:7; 12:6) that is the clue to his use of the Isaac story, since it is also applied to Isaac at Gen 22:2, 12, 16 (Greek text). The fact that Jewish tradition emphasised Isaac's free giving of himself in a sacrifice which took place on Mount Moriah, an old name for Jerusalem, at the passover, may also have influenced Mark's presentation. And even more striking still is the fact that the Greek text of Gen 22 says of Moriah 'On the mountain the Lord has been seen' (Gen 22:14). Thus the mount of sacrifice becomes the mount of revelation and, as we shall see, Mark exploits this idea to the full. On the basis of these considerations we would suggest the following tentative plan of the gospel as representing Mark's mind by the way he ordered his material. We shall follow this outline in the subsequent commentary.

INSCRIPTION: The good news of Jesus Christ, the Son of God (Mk 1 : 1).

INTRODUCTION (1 : 2–13): The bridge between the old and the new. John the Baptist's preaching (1 : 2–8); Jesus is baptised and is proclaimed the well-beloved Son (1 : 9–11) and the initial meeting of Jesus and Satan in the desert (1 : 12–13).

A. THE MYSTERY OF THE MESSIAH (In Galilee and beyond) Three sections, each *beginning* with a summary of the activity of Jesus and a narrative concerning the disciples and *concluding* with the adoption of an attitude in regard to Jesus.

1. *Jesus and the people* (1 : 14–3 : 6)
   (i) Introduction: summary of the preaching of the kingdom of God (1 : 14 f) and the call of the first disciples (1 : 16–20).
   (ii) A day's ministry at Capernaum (1 : 21–38) completed by a summary (1 : 39), an appendix, healing of a leper (1 : 40–44) and a further summary (1 : 45).
   (iii) Five controversies with scribes and Pharisees (2 : 1–3 : 5). In each case Jesus confounds his adversaries by a powerful saying and in the first and last by a miracle as well.
   (iv) Conclusion: the Pharisees decide to put Jesus to death (3 : 6).

2. *Jesus and his own* (3 : 7–6 : 6)
   (i) Introducton: a summary of healings and exorcisms (3 : 7–12) and the institution of the twelve (3 : 13–19).
   (ii) Narratives: Jesus is taken for a lunatic and a

demoniac. He proclaims the end of the empire of Satan, threatens unbelievers and declares who his true relatives are (3 : 20–35).

(iii) Parables: (4 : 1–34): parable of the sower (4 : 3–10); purpose for using parables (4 : 10–12); explanation of the parable of the sower (4 : 13–20); various parabolic sayings (4 : 21–25); two parables on the kingdom of God (4 : 26–32); conclusion (4 : 33–34).

(iv) Miracles: the stilling of the storm (4 : 35–41); the Gadarene demoniac (5 : 1–20); the daughter of Jairus and the woman with the issue of blood (5 : 21–43).

(v) Conclusion: rejection at Nazareth (6 : 1–5).

3. *Jesus and the disciples* (6 : 8–8 : 30)

(i) Introduction: summary of the teaching of Jesus (6 : 6), mission and return of the twelve enclosing the account of Herod's uneasiness and the death of John (6 : 7–30).

(ii) First multiplication of loaves (6 : 31–43) followed by a theophany at sea (6 : 44–52) and a summary of miracles in the land of Genesareth (6 : 53–56). Pharisees from Jerusalem come and there is a discussion about true cleanliness (7 : 1–23). Two miracles in the region of Tyre and Sidon (7 : 24–30) and in the midst of Decapolis (7 : 31–37), which may also be attached to the second multiplication of loaves.

(iii) Second multiplication of loaves (8 : 1–10) followed by a discussion with the Pharisees (8 : 11–13) and an instruction on the bread for the disciples (8 : 14–21).

(iv) Conclusion: the healing of a blind man at Bethsaida. (8 : 22–26; cf 10 : 46–52) and the confession of Peter (8 : 27–30). (This conclusion forms the transition to the second part of the gospel.)

B. THE MYSTERY OF THE SON OF MAN (Towards Jerusalem and in the city)

1. *The path of the Son of Man* (8:31–10:52)
It is signposted with three announcements of the fate of the Son of Man and three instructions on the fate of the disciples.

(i) First announcement: it is rejected by Peter who is described as Satan (8:31–33); teaching about true discipleship (8:35–9:1). Complement: the transfiguration and meeting with Elijah teach the same lesson (9:2–13); the healing of the epileptic shows Jesus' power over death (9:14–29).

(ii) Second announcement: journeying through Galilee (9:30–32). Teaching on service and some sayings (9:33–50). Further catechetical instruction on divorce, children, riches, and rewards of disciples (10:1–31). (This teaching takes place in Transjordan on the way up to Jerusalem.)

(iii) Third announcement: on the way up to Jerusalem (10:32–34); instruction for the disciples on the occasion of the request of the sons of Zebedee (10:35–45).

(iv) Conclusion: the Son of David is recognised by a blind man at Jericho (10:46–52; cf 8:22–26).

2. *The judgement on Jerusalem* (11:1–13:37)
(i) Judgement in act and word. Messianic entry (11:1–11), sellers are expelled from the temple (11:15–19), enclosed by the narrative concerning the barren fig tree (11:12–14, 20–25). Discussion on authority (11:27–33), concluded with the parable of the murderous husbandmen (12:1–12).

(ii) Controversies: tax to Caesar, resurrection of the dead, the first commandment, Christ, Son and Lord of

David, with the story of widow's mite as conclusion (12 : 13–44).

(iii) The *signs* and *time* of the destruction of the temple and the return of the Son of Man (13 : 1–37)

3. *Passion and resurrection* (14 : 1–16 : 8)

(i) Introduction : the plot and the treason enclosing the anointing at Bethany which underlines the drama of the death (14 : 1–11).

(ii) In secret : 'sacramental' preparation of the sacrifice and prayer in Gethsemane with a view to the hour (14 : 12–42).

(iii) In public : Jesus is arrested (14 : 43–52), condemned as messiah by the Jews (14 : 53–15 : 1) and as king by the pagans (15 : 2–20). Crucified, he dies and is recognised as the Son of God (cf 1 : 1) by the centurion, a gentile, before witnesses (15 : 21–41). He is buried (15 : 42–57).

(iv) Call to faith : the empty tomb (16 : 1–8).

(v) Epilogue : the appearance of the risen one and the command to preach the gospel (16 : 9–20).

3. Some dominant ideas of Mark's theology

In order to follow the thread of Mark's dramatic presentation it seems useful at the outset to give a brief summary of two key ideas that occur throughout the gospel as a whole and which serve to underline the distinctive features of the evangelist's insight into the person and work of Christ.

(a) *The demonic opposition to Jesus.* Late Jewish thought believed that in the act of creation God had overcome various powers of evil but that these had gradually reasserted themselves in the course of time. Accordingly, God would have to reaffirm his authority in a decisive

struggle against the evil powers before he could establish
his kingdom in a final way as he had promised. The evil
powers that were ranged against God's sovereign rule
manifested themselves in many different ways, not least
through demons or evil spirits who play such an important part in Mark's gospel. These evil spirits were united
under their leader Beelzebub or Satan and showed their
control over men's lives not just through possession but
also through sickness and other forms of physical and
mental disturbance. However, their real significance is
manifested in their opposition to God's kingly rule in
men's hearts. In Mark's view it is Satan who snatches the
seed of the word of God from a man's heart (4 : 15) and
consequently his opposition to the gospel message must
be destroyed if the mission of Jesus is to be successful.
This explains to a large degree the presence of the demonic in Mark's gospel and the deadly conflict between
Jesus and Satan that emerges. This conflict appears in
many different forms : the various exorcism narratives;
the temptation; the Beelzebub controversy; other nature
miracles; human opposition, whether it comes from controversy with opponents, opposition to his way from
Peter or blasphemy from his executioners. In face of
such opposition Jesus and his representatives have a twofold function in Mark's view, to expel demons and to
preach the gospel and these are obverse sides of the one
reality of God's kingdom at work in the world, provoking
the hostile forces to a last desperate stand against it. These
comments should help in understanding the basic thrust
of a large section of Mark's narrative, since the evangelist
sees Jesus' ministry as inaugurating this final onslaught
on the evil powers.

(b) *The messianic secret.* In 1901 a German new testament scholar called Wilhelm Wrede proposed an epoch-

making thesis regarding the secrecy motif that is such a feature of Mark's gospel. The explanation he gave to the data in question, namely that Mark is trying to vindicate the early church for attributing messiahship to Jesus, even though Jesus himself never claimed it, has not stood the test of time. But the data he has underlined certainly call for a positive interpretation in the light of Mark's overall theology. This is all the more necessary seeing that almost all the data in question are either omitted or given another interpretation by both Matthew and Luke.

The secrecy motif appears in several different ways throughout the gospel. There are the commands to silence issued to demons who profess his name (1 : 25, 34; 3 : 11 f), cured people (1 : 44; 5 : 43; 7 : 36; 8 : 26) and disciples (8 : 30; 9 : 8). The disciples are the recipients of special instruction 'in the house' (4 : 10; 7 : 17; 9 : 28, 33; 10 : 10), 'on the way' (1 : 33 f; 10 : 32, 52 f) or 'privately' (4 : 34; 6 : 31; 9 : 2, 28; 13 : 3). Jesus often seeks to be alone or to pass by without being recognised despite external enthusiasm from the crowd (7 : 24; 9 : 29). It has been suggested that Mark is only being faithful to the actual ministry of Jesus where such an attitude of secrecy would have been necessary in view of the demands for a political messiah in certain quarters. This explanation hardly does justice to the material, however, granted that Jesus must have had occasion to exercise caution with his over-zealous followers from time to time.

It is better to interpret this whole presentation in the light of Mark's understanding of what the true gospel is and what genuine faith in Jesus involves. The real content of the gospel does not concern Jesus the miracle-worker, or the one who expels demons, or even the Christ, but rather Jesus the crucified one who is risen as Son of God. Any understanding of him that leaves out the cross is in the end a false understanding in Mark's view. In fact acceptance of an empty title for Jesus without understanding what that title means in his life is part of Satan's opposition to the gospel and must be rejected. Enthusiastic adherence to Jesus just because of some favour he has granted is in reality no acceptance of him as a person. It merely uses Jesus because of his powers, and publicisation of these may only further obscure the real truth. Accordingly, true faith in Jesus must be prepared to accept him on his terms, that is as the crucified one. Only then will it lead to participation in the fate of Jesus and a share in his glory. That is why there can be no proclamation of Jesus before the cross and why the disciples, to whom the mystery is entrusted, must wait until after the resurrection before they can make it known (4:10, 25; 9:7). Prior to that even they do not fully understand its content.

Accordingly Mark brings us back to the pre-Easter life of the disciples with Jesus, not because he wishes to describe that period in detail, but rather because he invites his readers to come to a true faith in Jesus by way of the cross and thus enable them to understand what their own sonship of the common Father should mean. This is the only kind of faith that would stand the test for Mark's readers both then and now.

4. Mark's audience

Papias, an early witness, associates the gospel of Mark with Peter's preaching in Rome. According to this information, after the death of Peter in Nero's persecution (probably in the year 65 AD), Mark, being the apostle's interpreter, wrote down all that he could remember, not in order, but faithfully representing the apostle's teaching, which had been directed to the needs of his audience.

Other ancient witnesses such as Irenæus and Tertullian also situate the gospel in Rome and link it with Peter's preaching. Internal evidence shows that it was written for a non-Jewish audience (5:41; 7:3), and the number of latinisms, that is Latin words in Greek form, would also point towards Rome as its place of composition.

The link with Peter's preaching is particularly interesting since at Acts 10:37-41 Luke has preserved for us Peter's preaching in the house of a Roman at Caesarea, Cornelius, preaching that led to the baptism of this man and all his household. Even more interesting is the fact that these few verses could be regarded as a perfect outline of Mark's gospel. Peter stresses that Jesus 'went around doing good . . . healing all who were oppressed by the devil', an emphasis we have seen to be so central to Mark's gospel. The disciples as witnesses of the resurrection are said to 'have been chosen beforehand by God', something that Mark too stresses by emphasising the special place of the small group of the disciples 'with Jesus' from the time of their election (3:13). Finally, according to Mark it is a Roman centurion who first makes the full profession of faith (15:39), and Cornelius was a centurion!

We may therefore take the passage in Acts as an indication of the kind of audience Mark had in mind when writing his gospel. In all probability it was addressed to catechumens or new converts who had not yet fully appreciated all that their conversion and acceptance of the gospel involved. It was important for them to come to a mature understanding of their faith as quickly as possible because Nero's persecution of christians was now looming large on the horizon. They must understand the role of the cross in their lives as genuine followers of Jesus. This was what baptismal union with Christ meant, as Paul had

reminded the same Roman church a few years before
(Rom 6), and now they must be prepared to seal this
baptismal commitment by accepting his fate in order to
be recognised as true sons of his Father and co-heirs to
his glory (Rom 8:15–17). However, this is not just a
message for would-be Roman martyrs of the first century
AD. It is addressed to all those christians who wish to come
to an adult faith in Jesus as their crucified and risen
saviour. As they follow Mark's dramatic presentation of
the ministry of Jesus they are constantly being drawn
forward to the end in order to understand the gospel
fully. Their conceptions and ideas of what faith in Jesus
really implies are being purified all the time, until eventually they are drawn into the mystery of this death that
leads to life.

Book list for Mark and Matthew

S. Freyne, *The Twelve: Disciples and Apostles. An
Introduction to the Theology of the First Three Gospels*
1968.

D. E. Nineham, *Saint Mark* (Pelican Gospel Commentaries) 1963.

W. Barclay, *The First Three Gospels* London 1966.

R. H. Lightfoot, *The Gospel Message of Saint Mark*
1950.

V. Taylor, *The Gospel According to Saint Mark* 1963.

J. C. Fenton, *Saint Matthew* 1963.

W. Trilling, *The Gospel According to Saint Matthew*
1969.

C. H. Dodd, *The Parables of the Kingdom* 1935.

R. H. Fuller, *Interpreting the Miracles* 1963.

P. Benoit, *The Passion and Resurrection of Jesus* 1969.

1

Introductory passages
Mk 1:1–13

Mk 1:1. Descriptive title of the whole work

The word *euangelion*, 'good news', which Mark uses to introduce his work, means in profane Greek a good message or word such as the news of success in battle. It is often found with this meaning in the earlier books of the bible also. However with the anonymous prophet of the Babylonian captivity who is the author of Is 40–55 (c 530 BC), the word 'good news' and the related verb 'to announce the good news' take on a distinctively religious meaning (Is 40:9; 52:7). They refer to the great act of redemption that God is about to perform by freeing Israel from her Babylonian captivity. The good news refers to the victory of God yet to come. The new testament writers, especially Paul (Rom 1:17) and Mark, use the same word as a technical term to refer to the victory of God now ultimately achieved in Jesus Christ. In Rome where Mark was writing his gospel (the old English for 'good news') the word was used for such profane events as the birth of an emperor. Mark wishes to contrast such apparent and superficial good news with the real message of joy for man, that in and through Jesus God has conquered the forces of evil. As *good* news man is supposed to be vitally interested in the message, realising that since it concerns the most fundamental aspect of his life full

understanding can never be easy. From the start the
reader is invited to open his heart to this message which
vitally concerns him, and he must allow himself to be
drawn forward to the cross as the moment when the full
truth of the gospel emerges (15 : 39).

The gospel concerns Jesus Christ, the Son of God. He
is both the bringer of the good news and its content. Mark
illustrates this point subsequently by adding the phrase
'for the sake of the gospel' to sayings which speak of doing
something 'for the sake of Jesus' (8 : 35; 10 : 29). Jesus is
the gospel, and the gospel is Jesus, so that when a man
suffers for the gospel he is suffering for Jesus. When one
hears the gospel one is addressed by Jesus, as Mark shows
at 1 : 15 with Jesus' call: 'Repent and believe the gospel.'

Jesus is described as 'Jesus Christ, the Son of God'. We
are so familiar with the name 'Jesus Christ' that it may
surprise us to hear that 'Christ' was not originally a
proper name at all, but literally means 'the anointed one'
in Greek. This in turn was a translation of its Hebrew
equivalent 'the messiah', that is the expected redeemer
that God would send at the end of time to save his people.
As the anointed one he was to be endowed with special
power and under the particular protection of God. As
time went on this saving role of the messiah was conceived differently by different groups of the people, a
political liberator being one very popular understanding
of his mission at the time of Jesus. The important thing
was that whenever people spoke of the messiah they never
thought of it as a name but as a role or mission to be accomplished, however differently that mission was envisaged. Mark is well aware of this original derivation of the
name 'Christ' (8 : 29; 12 : 35; 13 : 21 f) so the fact that he
can use it as a proper name is not just a piece of historical
forgetfulness of the original derivation. Rather he is say-

ing something profoundly important about Jesus by adding 'Christ' as another name. He is attesting to the fact that Jesus fulfilled the role of messiah so uniquely that his role becomes his name. Unfortunately, as we will see, many of those who were attracted to him initially would have been content had he given himself less completely to his role, and so fulfilled their messianic dreams of power and authority. Now, however, if they are to remain his followers they must give themselves to their vocation as he has done, and that is never easy.

Jesus' giving of himself to his messianic task merited for him a new name and this meant that he must have been specially dear to God and specially anointed by him. That is why Mark adds another title for Jesus, 'Son of God', at the outset. Again this title was capable of realisation at different levels, for Israel could be described as God's son, as were the kings after their enthronement, and angelic messengers. The early church saw Jesus' resurrection as his enthronement and thus he realises this title in a unique and special way, by comparison with which the enthronement of Israel's kings was a very pale shadow. He had entered into a new and definitive relationship with God through his resurrection, and so manifested a level of communion between God and his Son never before realised. Thus what was now a title of honour for him was previously a challenge and a vocation (Rom 1:1-4). Mark in introducing his work uses 'Son of God' for Jesus as a title of honour but subsequently it will emerge that it was first of all a cross to carry. It is his favourite designation for Jesus, provided both aspects, the vocation and the glory, are properly understood. Shortly the voice from heaven will describe Jesus as 'My well beloved Son', and this immediately implies that he must share his Father's concern for mankind. As a God of love and concern he will soon share his Spirit with Jesus and that will mean that Jesus will be consumed by the same love and concern, setting off on his ministry to 'do good because God was with him' (Acts 10 : 38).

1. *How best can you prepare yourself to hear the good news that is Mark's gospel story?*

2. *Explain the full significance of the name 'Jesus Christ'.*

3. *Why did Mark prefer the title 'Son of God' for Jesus, yet use it so sparingly?*

Mk 1:2–13. Introduction: the chief actors in the drama

(a) *John and his message.* The Baptist is introduced through the words of Isaiah and Malachi as the herald who makes suitable arrangements for the arrival of the monarch. He begins his activity in the desert, a place where hostile forces dwell, as Jesus is soon to learn. Yet the longed for messiah was to appear there first, as is evidenced by the Qumran community waiting for his arrival by the shores of the Dead Sea. John does not proclaim the good news, but merely calls for repentance or a change of heart from his audience. Like the prophet Elijah, whose style of life he imitates, and who is expected to herald the messianic times (Mal 4:5; Mk 9:11), he is aware that men will not accept the good news of salvation unless they have a lively sense of need for it based on the realisation of their own sinfulness.

(b) *The baptism and temptation of Jesus.* The author of the last part of the book of Isaiah expressed a keenly felt desire of later Israel when he prayed: 'Oh that you would tear the heavens open and come down' (Is 64: 1). It was

generally believed that there would be an extraordinary
outpouring of God's Spirit at the end time. God's spirit
was God's life bestowed on man, giving him life and
energy and the possibility of responding to God's grace
in accordance with his vocation 'made in the image of
God' (Gen 1 : 27). It was through his spirit that God had
conquered the chaos at the beginning and shared his life
with man by breathing on the dust of the earth, so that
man became 'a living self' (Gen 2 : 7). In the new creation
of the end of days there would have to be a similar activity
of God's spirit (Ezek 36 : 36). This same spirit of God
was also particularly active during the long course of
Israel's history in helping judges, kings and prophets to
fulfil their divinely appointed vocations on behalf of
God's people. The messiah was expected to be particularly endowed in this regard (Is 11 : 1–10), an endowment
that could be described as an anointing (Is 61 : 1–3). We
know that Peter addressing the house of Cornelius spoke
of Jesus being anointed with the Holy Spirit and with
power, and it was this anointing that enabled him to engage in the conflict with Satan and go around doing good
(Acts 10 : 37 f), God's presence was with him through this
special relationship, for God never asks anybody to perform a task without giving the strength to accomplish it.

Jesus identifies himself with sinful humanity by undergoing John's purificatory rite. Mark reports the matter
quite frankly with no protestations of unworthiness on
the part of the Baptist, as in Matthew's account. It is Jesus
who sees the heavens opened and to him alone the
heavenly voice is addressed. It is as though Jesus is being
called to fulfil his vocation as Son by being the *well-
beloved* Son after the pattern of Isaac who was prepared
to sacrifice his life to ensure the blessings of God for
mankind (Gen 22 : 2, 12, 16). Jesus too will go to Mount

Moriah, an old name for Jerusalem, and his love-filled offering of himself on behalf of mankind will reveal him for what he really is, the well-beloved Son of a loving Father. Then the words of Isaac's father, Abraham, will be fulfilled : 'On the mount the Lord has been seen' (Gen 22 : 14 LXX). At once the Spirit which descends on Jesus starts him on the road that leads to that self-giving and self-revelation by driving him out to the desert to meet Satan, his great adversary in Mark's presentation. We are not told the outcome of this first encounter between Jesus and Satan, but the presence of the wild beasts recalls the taming of nature, one of the victories of the messianic age according to the prophet Isaiah (Is 11 : 1–9). Yet the ministry of angels anticipates Jesus' agony before the passion (cf Lk 22 : 43). From the start this victory of Jesus over the powers of evil makes its full demands on him.

1. What is the role of the Spirit in the life of Jesus?

2. What is the significance of Jesus' identification with sinful humanity for a proper understanding of his redemptive work? (See Heb 2 : 14–18; 2 Cor 5 : 16–19.)

3. How can the church today respond to the challenge it poses for it to do likewise?

2

Scene one: Jesus and the people
Mk 1:14–3:6

After this introduction to the chief actors and the nature
of the drama, the first act begins to unfold in three
scenes: Jesus presents himself as the saviour and healer
of the people at large (1 : 14–3 : 6), 'his own' (3 : 7–6 : 6),
and his disciples (6 : 6–8 : 29). Eventually Peter on behalf
of the disciples alone recognises him as the messiah.

In the first scene we get a good-cross section of Jesus'
activity among the people, 'going around doing good'.
Mark presents us with a number of isolated and colourful
pictures of Jesus dealing with individuals, interspersed
with short summary statements of fact. This helps to give
the overall effect of universal coverage and at the same
time the narrative never becomes cold or impersonal.
However opposition soon begins to mount against Jesus,
and despite his ability to settle the issues raised by a
powerful word or deed the decision of the religious and
political leaders to put him to death is inevitable. This
leads to the second scene where Jesus turns to the smaller
group of disciples centred on the twelve. Indeed their
election is the consequence of the decision of the authorities despite the continued excitement and attraction of
the crowd. The disciples are described as his 'true relatives'; whereas his own say that he is mad. Throughout

23

this section of parables (chapter 4) and miracles (chapter 5) the real attention is focussed on the disciples despite the fact that the crowd remain present and are taught 'insofar as they are able to understand'. The final separation of Jesus and his own comes with the rejection of Jesus at Nazareth. The third scene concentrates even more on the disciples. They are sent on mission to experience personally the power entrusted to them by Jesus. Afterwards, they are in the desert with Jesus and they see how he can fulfil the needs of the people with bread like Yahweh of old. Yet they are almost as obtuse as the people at large in failing to grasp the real significance of Jesus and his work. It is only after repeated instruction that eventually Peter can make the profession 'Thou art the Christ'.

Mk 1:14 f. The arrival of Jesus and his preaching about the kingdom

In these few verses Mark succeeds in bringing together some of the key ideas of his work. The departure of John the Baptist is the clue for Jesus to begin his life's work for men as a herald of the good news. The Greek word for 'preaching' means literally to act as a herald, that is the official town crier who made known to the public the news of greatest concern to them. The herald had a particularly important part to play in time of war, when news of victory or defeat meant the difference between life and death for people. It was not the herald's function to delay or argue about the good news, but rather to proclaim it far and wide so that all might share in its joy. Mark succeeds in giving us such a picture of Jesus and his ministry. This 'kerygmatic' approach serves his purpose well, for it succeeds in arousing our interest, and

causing us to question our presuppositions and our attitudes. If we miss the excitement that the message gener-
ates then we suddenly find ourselves isolated, others may
already be celebrating!

The content of Jesus' message concerns the kingdom of
God. In chapter 4 we shall learn more about this concept
and its manner of manifesting itself in the world, but
here we must try to grasp something of its original meaning and force. When modern man thinks of a kingdom,
he immediately thinks of a territory with its boundaries,
officials and various institutions. However the ancient
world approached these matters much more pragmati-
cally because life was not so stabilised or structured then
as it is now. A king's territory extended only as far as his
rule ran. Thus the primary emphasis is always on the
king's rule rather than the territory where this is operative. This is particularly true of the kingdom of God
which Jesus preached. The immediate background is that
of late Jewish apocalyptic, a type of literature which
emerged in the last two centuries before Christ to console
and encourage faithful Jews who were being persecuted
for their loyalty to faith and fatherland. In general the
message of apocalyptic saw God's kingdom as a totally
new intervention on behalf of his people. Ideas such as
resurrection of the dead and new creation emerge in this
literature and there are descriptions of cosmic upheavals,
signs and wonders. The basic theological idea underlying
all these descriptions is the belief that for the religious
situation of man to be changed and the evil that is inherent in that situation to be destroyed there is need for
a drastic intervention by God in human history which
would eradicate the forces of evil and establish his kingly
rule whereby men could live in peace and harmony.
Thus apocalyptic took up the basic thrust of Israel's cove-

nant theology, namely that God is faithful to his promises
and in the end all would be well for his people.

The idea of the kingdom of God is absolutely central
to Jesus' preaching, and the term appears in all 104 times
on his lips in the gospels. For him the final act of salvation
was taking place in and through his ministry. The time
was fulfilled in the sense that the speculation about how
soon the kingdom of God would manifest itself, so characteristic of Jewish apocalyptic, was now over. God was at
last inaugurating his kingly rule in a final and ultimate
way and the powers of evil were about to be destroyed
definitively. It was not just that a certain point in time
had been reached, but rather that the period of waiting
was over; the old world had run its course and God's
giving of himself to the world had reached its high-point
and man's opportunity was at its maximum. There is one
very important difference, however, between Jesus' understanding of the kingdom and that of late Jewish apocalyptic, no matter how much his conceptions were grounded
in such ideas. A comparison with John the Baptist is
illuminating here. For John God's kingdom is coming
now as judgement: 'now the axe is laid to the root of the
tree', but with Jesus it is present as pure grace and forgiveness. Jesus does not remove the note of urgency in
regard to the kingdom and man's response to it, but he
does change the emphasis. The kingdom, for Jesus, is
manifested in and through the lowliness of his own ministry, for God is ready to stay his judging hand and to
accede to the request 'let it alone this year also, lest perhaps it bring forth fruit'. Thus in the preaching of Jesus
the kingdom of God is a personal call rather than an
apocalyptic manifestation, and this was part of the scandal
of his claim. But such a call only made sense when God
was already offering himself to man as the ground and

source of his fulfilment. However, to accept such an offer man must be prepared to surrender his own pretentions; he must have a change of heart, for he has never desired any other kingly rule except his own ambitions ever since Adam, that is man the sinner, chose the serpent's way in the beginning.

The call of Jesus was not just a detached piece of ethical reasoning, but a deep personal conviction, based on the experience of his own life. For him too the kingdom of God was present as his Father's intimate presence and the demands this made on him as the well-beloved Son. Jesus could tell others to follow him with the utmost assurance that his way was the true way to acceptance of the kingdom: if you would enter into life 'follow me' (Mk 10:17–22). So total was Jesus' self-giving that to believe the good news about him and accept the radical implications of discipleship with him was identical with submitting oneself to the kingly rule of God that he preached. Mark sees the inner connection that exists between the gospel about Jesus that he is presenting to the reader and the good news of the kingdom that Jesus preached in his own lifetime. It is the same good news in terms of God's self-giving and the radical demands that this imposed on man. Thus at the very outset the reader is assured that Mark's presentation is faithful to the only good news there is: God's victory is now.

1. What does the kingdom of God mean to you?

2. Explain the difference between John the Baptist's and Jesus' understanding of the kingdom.

3. What is the connection between the kingdom as gift and as challenge?

4. Explain the identity between Mark's message and the good news of the kingdom preached by Jesus.

Mk 1:16–20. The call of the first disciples

Like every other wandering teacher of his day Jesus was
surrounded by a fairly permanent band of followers. The
practice was that a person attached himself to a particular
teacher as his disciple, attending to the master's needs
and receiving in return the instruction in the *torah* which
would entitle him to become an independent teacher one
day. There are two important differences, however, between the disciples of Jesus and those of other late Jewish
rabbis. Entry into his circle was the result of his invitation, 'come follow me', and there was never a question of
graduation from his retinue: 'Be not you called teacher,
one is your teacher, the Christ' (Mt 23:10). This meant
that Jesus could never be regarded as just another rabbi,
no matter how much his outward style and appearance
resembled such, because Jesus spoke in his own name and
by his own authority, not as an *interpreter* of what Moses
had said. Thus following of Jesus as his disciple now involved implicit acceptance of him and his claims, and
willingness to serve him, not a right to independent status
apart from him. The early church retained this picture
of the first band of Jesus' followers literally leaving all to
follow him, because it illustrated so concretely what was
now expected of all believers in their radical commitment
to Christ, despite the fact that Jesus was no longer physically present in their midst. Thus the stories of the call
of the first disciples are shorn of all unnecessary bio-
graphical or psychological detail to highlight the call of
Christ and the response the christian should make. Mark,
by presenting the call of the two pairs of brothers at this
point, wishes to illustrate for his readers what repentance
and believing the gospel just announced would mean in
practice. The follower does not yet know the full impli-

cations of his decision, but he is prepared to trust the master and is willing to go wherever he leads. The subsequent story of these and the other disciples' failures and disillusionments will put careful readers on their guard against any facile acceptance of their own call and safeguard against disappointments that may lie ahead.

1. What does this vocation story imply about faith in Jesus today?

2. How can the lay christian 'leave all' to follow Jesus?

Mk 1:21–45. A typical day in the ministry of Jesus

The original proclamation of Jesus about the kingdom takes place in public, and Mark continues his description of Jesus' dealing with the crowds by outlining a typical day in the ministry. The emphasis throughout is on the healing nature of Christ's work, embracing the spiritual and intellectual ills of mankind just as much as the physical needs. The people are immediately attracted to Jesus since his authority or, perhaps better, his authenticity is apparent by contrast with the scribes, the official teachers of the law. This is the first of several comments that Mark makes about the quality of Jesus' teaching, but he rarely delays to give us any examples, since all attention must be focussed on his person, as is clear in the three incidents which follow.

(i) *Confrontation with a demoniac.* In this scene the question of the superior power of Jesus is central, something the demon recognises by his question, 'Are you come to destroy us?', and his confidence in resisting this threat by knowing Jesus' name as the holy one of God. Such knowledge was believed to give special power over an adversary in the ancient world. Thus the struggle begun in the desert must continue, and the outcome of this first public skirmish—Jesus commands the unclean spirit to depart—shows where the ultimate victory will lie, even if mankind must suffer, torn and convulsed for a time like this poor demoniac.

What should the victory of Christ over the forces of evil in the world mean for christians?

(ii) *Some cures.* The cure of Peter's mother-in-law is the prelude to a demonstration of Jesus' power over all forms of sickness and possession. There is a striking contrast between the public performance and that which takes place in the house in the presence of those already called to follow. In this latter instance Jesus takes the woman by the hand and *raises her up,* an anticipated sharing of his resurrection power, to which she responds by ministering to him as the first deaconess of the church. The people outside on the other hand are excited and involved, but there is no indication of understanding or willingness to serve.

What does this story tell you about the sacraments as acts of Christ and the correct response of christians?

(iii) *Jesus at prayer.* Jesus' rather sudden departure before daybreak may appear surprising, but clearly he is disappointed with the reaction of the crowd. Communion with his Father will give him the courage to continue despite this initial failure, but he is not interested in the search for him, nor does he share the enthusiasm of Simon and those who were with him for the crowd's attitude. They are not yet called disciples since they share the people's attraction for this fascinating wonder-worker, not realising that genuine faith means following Jesus in lowliness, even to the giving up of one's life in order to save it. Genuine discipleship means abandoning our human concerns and preoccupations, even about God, and accepting the fact that we are totally dependent on him for our existence. We must be ready to let go of ourselves as we are in order to discover our true selves with him.

1. How does the prayer of Jesus indicate an attitude to prayer that is relevant today and a role for prayer in our daily lives?

2. What particular aspect of our christian vocation is highlighted by the description 'followers of Christ'?

(iv) *Conclusion.* Jesus is not prepared to return to Capernaum since his mission from the Father is to all men. Nobody, not even his mother or his chosen disciples, have an exclusive claim on him. He therefore continues his journey through Galilee preaching, no doubt about the kingdom, and casting out demons, that is continuing the struggle already begun. The cure of a leper serves as an example of his healing ministry on this tour. Jesus' command for silence, the first of several similar injunctions in the gospel, shows his unwillingness to be cast in the role of a popular, wonder-working hero, since that is not the correct way to understand his radical message for mankind. Any publicisation of him from this point of view could only impede a correct appreciation of how he proposes to 'save' men. The concluding summary leaves us with a picture of the crowds still flocking after him enthusiastically despite his best efforts to avoid such euphoria.

1. What is the significance of Jesus' reply to Simon?
2. Explain the command to keep the miracle silent.

Mk 2:1–3:6. The beginnings of controversy

Even though Mark has confined himself to describing
only one day of the ministry he has succeeded in painting
a picture of extensive activity on the part of Jesus. He
has covered the whole region and has been enthusiastically received by the crowd, if only as a wonder-worker.
Soon opposition begins to mount against him from those
whose position of authority and influence is threatened
by his presence, namely, the official religious and political
leaders. They have perceived something more about him
and his mission than the crowd, but lack their unpre-
judiced good will. This section consists of five controversies between Jesus and such opponents, in all of which his
critics are confounded by a word of Jesus reflecting a
definite break with their attitudes and a comment on his
own life, and by a miracle as well in the first and last
instance. The only effect of such confrontations is to
harden the opposition to Jesus, culminating in the decision to put him to death (3 : 6).

(i) *2 : 1–12. The cure of the paralytic.* The question of
sin loomed large in the life of the late Jewish community.
Yahweh had punished Israel for its unfaithfulness and
the post-exilic community (ie judaism after the return
from Babylon in 521 BC) was extremely conscious of its
sinfulness, both community (Neh 9 : 6–38; Dan 9 : 3–19)
and personal (Ezek 17; Ps 51). Consequently, the messianic age was seen as a time when Israel would be totally
free of sin—Yahweh himself would wipe it away and ensure that his people would be faithful (Jer 31 : 31 ff; Ezek
36 : 22–32). Jesus showed his real concern for sinners by
accepting fellowship with them and sharing a common
table with those whom the self-righteous religious leaders
regarded as sinners (Mk 2 : 17). In adopting such an atti-

tude he considered himself true to the kingdom of God
which he preached and many of his parables tell of the
joy of God at the return of the sinner (cf Lk 15). The
christian community shared the same concern for sin and
the sinner in its midst (eg 1 Cor 5:5; Mt 18:14–16) while
at the same time not losing sight of its true vocation to be
the sinless community of messianic times (1 Jn 3:4–10).

These considerations form the background to this story,
which is much more concerned with Jesus and his attitude to sin, an attitude shared by the early church, than
it is with the cure of the paralytic, impressive as this
latter event may appear to our eyes today. For those who
brought the sick man to Jesus, his initial statement, 'your
sins are forgiven you' had a very natural ring since for all
Jews there was an intimate connection between sin and
physical suffering, a connection that the book of Job
queries in highly dramatic fashion without being able
to offer any positive solution in its place. Jesus however,
did not accept such a combination (Jn 9:3) and his statement 'Thy sins are forgiven thee' had an absolute quality
of its own. However on seeing the challenge to his statement by the religious leaders he decides to accept them
on their own terms, and by curing the paralytic vindicates
his original claim, which implied that Jesus spoke on
behalf of God in regard to sin. Thus the early church in
conducting its ministry to the sinner considered that its
powers were based on the authority of Jesus (Mt 18:18;
Jn 20:23) whose messianic mission it was called on to
continue in the world.

*1. What does the role of the friends of the paralytic
imply for the community nature of sin and forgiveness?*
*2. How could the church express such an understand-
ing in its life and liturgy?*

3. In your opinion is there any connection between sin and sickness?

(ii) *2:13–17. The call of Levi.* This story follows very naturally on the previous one, and no doubt Mark has positioned it here in order to illustrate Jesus' determination to show his care for sinners despite the 'scandal' and opposition of the scribes, the official interpreters of the law. The call of Levi follows the same pattern as the previous vocation story, except that now he is described as a 'tax-collector'. This profession was associated with the hated Roman rule and regarded as a betrayal of Jewish religious beliefs, and as well it was open to all kinds of unjust abuses. Tax-collectors and sinners were almost synonymous in the eyes of a 'pious' Jew (see 2:15 f). Not only does Jesus call such a man to join his retinue, but further shares his table in his house, a sure sign for an oriental of mutual trust and friendship. Jesus makes a devastating reply to his indignant, self-righteous opponents. His ministry is a healing one, directed at the outcasts and those who have the basic honesty to recognise their need for help. It is only these who can benefit from him or the gift of God that he offers. The self-righteous who think that they alone know the way to God have by their attitude cut themselves off from God's self-giving which now confronts them in Jesus.

1. How could the idea of a meal as a sign of reconciliation between two parties be used by the church today in its healing ministry?

2. How can the attitude of the self-righteous scribes be a real danger for christian belief now?

(iii) *2:18–22. The question of fasting.* Fasting was a work of supererogation especially dear to pious Jews (Mt 6:16–

18) and should Jesus and his followers adopt an unconventional line towards such practices they would soon be marked off from their contemporaries of more strict observance. The reply of Jesus here is that fasting does have a place in the christian dispensation but it must be motivated now by the taking away of the bridegroom, that is the messiah, according to Jewish expectation. For the christian, then, it is one way of identifying with the death of Christ. In writing to the same Roman converts Paul insists that their baptism commits them to dying with Christ (Rom 6 : 3–6), and the motivation for fasting given here is in line with such general instruction. Two other sayings of Jesus dealing with the impossibility of mixing the old and the new emphasise the fact that for Christians a radical break with the past and its attitudes is called for, even when they engage in the same kind of religious practices as their Jewish neighbours, for a whole new spirit has come into human life with Jesus.

1. What is the role of fasting in christian asceticism today?

2. Where does the church still cling on to 'old' attitudes in its life and practice?

(iv) *2 : 23–28. Dispute about the sabbath.* The sabbath observance was one particularly sacrosanct Jewish custom, as is clear from the fact that it was sanctioned by God the creator in the beginning (Gen 2 : 2 f). The extent to which their legalism had gone is clear from their objection to the disciples of Jesus plucking ears of grain as they passed by the edge of a corn field, since all work was prohibited on that day. Jesus begins his reply in best rabbinical style by citing examples from their own scriptures, where contrary custom seemed to have operated. This would be a usual ploy between two rabbis discussing such a case. The scribes' pondering of the case Jesus puts to them only leaves them more vulnerable to his real answer —the sabbath was intended to serve man, not to enslave him. And then a final saying about the Son of Man as lord of the sabbath really drives home his point. As yet the Son of Man, a mysterious other-world figure of Jewish apocalyptic, has not been positively identified with Jesus, something that will take place through his suffering, as we shall see. For the moment, though, the linking of the mysterious Son of Man with men whom the sabbath is intended to serve only creates further disarray in their ranks.

1. What is the role of the christian sabbath?

2. How can legalism in regard to practices and customs destroy the true spirit of religion?

(v) *3 : 1–6. Another cure.* The sabbath is still the centre of controversy in this section, and carries Jesus' criticism of their attitudes further, by indicating an obvious example of when the demand of God would call for violation of the sabbath law as they understand it. Jesus' straightforward question confounds his critics but does not convert them. They are so smug in their self-righteous observances that in order to fulfil the letter of the law they would be prepared to deny a fundamental principle of human life, that a man should try to save life, not destroy it. By contrasting this basic principle with their legalism Jesus clearly shows that there is a genuine hierarchy of moral values, and that God does not expect legalistic worship when real service of one's fellow man is called for.

Jesus' reaction is one of sorrow and anger, by no means contradictory emotions in a situation where he desires so earnestly to convince them and change their attitude. He is grieved at their 'hardness of heart', a word with a long history in the bible. It covers a number of different attitudes towards God and his revelation: blindness, stubborness and refusal to see something that is patently obvious to all unbiased viewers.

1. When is anger a legitimate christian reaction to a situation?

2. How would hardness of heart manifest itself among religious people today?

3

Scene two: Jesus and his own
Mk 3:7–6:6

In this section we witness the gradual separation of the true followers of Jesus from the crowds at large. The genuine disciples turn out to be 'those whom he would himself', and not, as might have been expected, his blood relations or his fellow townsmen.

Mk 3:7-12. Introduction: a general summary

Large crowds, including some gentiles, come to Jesus by the seashore 'hearing all that he did'. The word of the good news is always important in drawing people to the master. These crowds from Palestine and outside may well have symbolised for Mark the future mission of the church. At the same time a boat is ready 'lest the crowd crush him'. He may have to withdraw from them if their adherence to him is of the wrong type and of such extent that he would be submerged by them, thereby inhibiting his real ministry to men. Yet clearly such enthusiasm shows an open-mindedness which is such a fertile mission ground for the church. This setting may well have been consciously intended by Mark as the background to the election of the twelve to form the nucleus of the apostolic community whose task it will be to carry on the true ministry of Jesus in the world. Once again such a meeting between Jesus and the world brings out the forces of evil inherent in it, as the demons, threatened by Jesus' healing and saving presence, try to avoid open confrontation with him by worshipping him and professing his name. They know his correct name, something that is hidden from men until the cross (15:39), but of course their utterance of it does not imply acceptance of him or a true appreciation of his person. Jesus will not be tempted by such demonic opposition to the true gospel he has to preach and so commands silence, thereby showing his mastery over them (cf 1:24 f; 5:7).

1. What does this passage teach about the mission of the church in the world?

2. Explain the demons' reactions and Jesus' command to silence.

Mk 3:13–19. Election of the twelve

The very location of this scene, the mountain, serves to distinguish it sharply from the previous one by the seashore. In the old testament, the mountain is a place of special revelation, and it is from there that Yahweh addresses Moses to inaugurate the original covenant with his people (Ex 19). Subsequently, after Moses has ratified the covenant with an altar of twelve pillars 'for the twelve tribes of Israel' he ascends the mountain with the elders of the people there to meet their covenant-God face to face (Ex 24). Such a background forms the setting for the event of special significance that Mark now wishes to narrate, the election of the twelve as the nucleus of the community that is destined to be the people of the new covenant.

The number twelve had a very special significance because it recalled the twelve founding fathers of the twelve tribes, the sons of Jacob, who made up the original Israel. The number twelve itself probably goes back to the days of a central sanctuary in Israel, when each tribe was responsible for looking after the shrine with its relics of the liberation such as the ark of the covenant, for one month each year. The names of the tribes can vary from one list to another within the old testament but the number twelve itself is sacrosanct as constitutive of Israel the covenant people. In the centuries after the schism between the ten northern tribes and those of the south in 910 BC the idea of re-unification of 'all Israel' as the covenant people became a burning religious and political issue despite the fact that a state of war often existed between the two groups. This was further intensified after the fall of Samaria and the taking away of the northern tribes by Assyria in 721 BC. Any immediate hope of return and re-unification was lost, and so the idea was transferred to the end-time and became one of the expressions of hope for the time when God would eventually fulfil all his covenant promises for Israel. In the period between the two testaments there is scarcely an extant Jewish book that has not some expression of the idea of the reunification of the twelve tribes as part of the restoration of messianic times.

It is against this background that we must understand the call of the twelve by Jesus, for he has explicitly linked them with 'the twelve tribes of Israel' (Mt 19:28; Lk 20:30). Given such a link, Jesus was in effect declaring that his community with its twelvefold structure was in fact the messianic community of Jewish expectation. As in the old testament, the number twelve is sacrosanct even though the lists of names do not tally completely, and the discrepancies cannot just be explained by variations on the names of the same people. The fact that the first act of the apostolic community recorded by Luke is the election of Matthias to the place of Judas (Acts 1:15–26) is a further indication of the constitutive and symbolic role the twelve played in the life of that community in expressing both its self-understanding and its vocation. As such there is no need to re-elect the college in each generation, provided its original symbolic role is remembered. We tend to speak automatically of the twelve apostles, and there is no doubt that the group was entrusted with and did subsequently exercise the apostolic office, even though others such as Paul and Barnabas could also share these same apostolic functions (Acts 14:4; 1 Cor 9:1; 15:8). At the same time it should be recognised that the expression 'the twelve apostles' is rare in the new testament (Mt 10:2) and the designation of the twelve as apostles is of interest only to Luke, it would seem (Lk 6:13–19). On the other hand, the group is known as 'the twelve', simply, from a very early stage (1 Cor 15:5); and it is necessary to make some distinction between the two designations. As 'the twelve' simply the emphasis is certainly on the community aspect, that is their symbolic role as indicating that the community of Jesus is the messianic community. This does not preclude certain individuals within the group from receiving special functions, as is clear from the name-giving motif which Mark has introduced with the list of twelve names here. Yet the emphasis is heavily on their community aspect, something Mark demonstrates by practically identifying the twelve and the disciples as the permanent followers of Jesus (see 11:11, 14; 14:12, 14, 17). They are 'to be with him' as the community that understands Jesus, his ministry and his person. Subsequently in the gospel Mark concentrates almost exclusively on this aspect of their call and they are made the recipients of

private instruction, away from the sympathetic and interested yet undiscerning crowd.

Yet Mark is also aware of the true meaning of an
apostle as the duly legitimated representative of Jesus,
whose task it is to carry on the essence of Jesus' ministry
as 'the one who is sent'. After their mission in Galilee he
reports that the apostles returned telling all that they had
done and taught (6:30) even though, as we shall see, Mark
treats that particular mission with some reserve. Because
of their inadequate understanding of Jesus at that point
they cannot yet be his full representatives, but the present
passage makes it clear that they are intended to fulfil that
function eventually. They are to be sent 'to preach' and
'to have power to cast out demons', two aspects of Jesus'
total ministry as Mark has presented it (1:14, 38 f; 1:24,
39). These are intimately connected aspects, since as we
have seen in the introduction, the activity of the evil one
was considered to be particularly intensive at the dawning
of the messianic age. Mark sees this activity in terms of
hostility to the gospel message, either in trying to snatch
the seed that was sown (4:15), or obstructing the way to
true revelation (8:33), or even attempting to proclaim
Jesus as Son of God without acceptance or understanding
of what this involved (3:12). Always Satan and the gospel
are opposed, and there is every reason for those who are
charged with its future proclamation to be empowered
to destroy those forces that are opposed to its being understood and accepted. True, Mark does not concentrate
very much on this, the apostolic aspect of the twelve's
vocation, and their future world-wide mission is only
hinted at (4:22; 9:9; 13:10; 14:9). Still by introducing
the idea now Mark shows how a correct understanding
of the apostolate, and a proper exercise of its office should
develop from and grow out of a community that is centred

on Jesus and accepts him fully as the source of its life
and strength. The apostle is merely the extension of the
community's life, faith and understanding.

1. How can the church today be faithful to Jesus' in-
tention of giving his community a twelvefold structure?
2 What is the connection between an apostle and his
community?
3. Describe ways in which you consider Satan is op-
posed to the gospel today.

Mk 3:20–35. A wrong understanding of Jesus and his ministry

This passage provides a striking contrast to the previous
one. Jesus called whom he would himself to be members
of the twelve, and their willingness to answer his call can
be compared with the attitude of the friends who say that
he is mad (which is equivalent to having a demon, according to Jn 10:20 f) and that of the scribes who say that
he is in league with Satan. The friends of Jesus (or 'his
relations'; the Greek is imprecise) are distressed because
of his rejection of conventional attitudes in regard to
social barriers and religious practices. Their reaction is
totally human and natural and shows that they have not
even begun to ask the correct question that might lead
to faith in Jesus. Indeed their reaction to Jesus was such
an embarrassment that the other two evangelists have left
it out altogether. Mark specifies these relations further
as 'your mother and your brothers' towards the end of the
section (3:31–35), and Jesus is given the opportunity to
make a clear distinction between blood relationship with
him and the true relationship of faith and following. The
understanding of christians as brothers of Jesus was

deeply embedded in the early church (Mt 25:40; Heb
2:11 f). It was a source of confidence on the one hand
because they could with Jesus address God as Father,
'Abba' (Rom 8:15), and at the same time it was the
motive for observing the law of brotherly love. Being
brothers of Jesus implied that a spirit of brotherhood
should prevail within the community (Acts 2:43–47).
For Jesus such a spirit had nothing to do with blood kinship but derived rather from acceptance of God's will
(exemplified by following of Jesus) as the only true
direction for one's life. Mark does not necessarily see
Jesus as rejecting Mary here, but rather as indicating that
her relationship with him as bringer of God's kingdom
must now be of a different kind, something John indicates
in a more subtle fashion by describing Mary's role at
Cana and at the foot of the cross (Jn 2:1–11, 19:25–27).

On the other hand Jesus' reaction to the scribes is
swift and decisive. Mark says that he replied to them 'in
parables', because his reply typifies the mysterious nature
of his person and the utter impossibility for those outside
to appreciate him, as is illustrated in 'the parable chapter'
to follow (Mk 4). His first answer is that if what they say
is true, namely that he is in league with Satan, then the
reign of Satan is over, since no house or kingdom divided
against itself can stand. Secondly, he uses the image of
binding to describe the power over Satan which Jesus,
'the stronger one' to whom the Baptist referred (1:7),
possesses. By a strange paradox this victory of Jesus was
achieved through his death, which Mark portrays in the
light of Isaac's sacrifice, something later judaism described 'as the binding of Isaac'. Jesus' ultimate victory
over Satan was achieved through his death and resurrection (cf Heb 2:14 ff), but in Mark's account this ultimate victory is anticipated in the temptation and exor-

cism narratives. This anticipated victory of Jesus is brought about by the power of the Spirit who first drove him to confront Satan (1:12). To attribute Jesus' success to any source other than the Spirit of God would be the ultimate blasphemy, 'an everlasting sin'. The rabbis often classified certain sins as unworthy of forgiveness, thereby stressing the fact that one should not place too much trust in God's infinite mercy. Perhaps this saying of Jesus should be seen against that background. In Mark's view the whole ministry of Jesus is so divinely inspired that it could only be 'from God' and anybody who would think otherwise must have his mind so closed to the truth that they could never understand.

1. How might christians today share the attitude of Jesus' blood relations to him?

2. Explain why blasphemy against the Holy Spirit is an everlasting sin.

Mk 4:1–33. Jesus teaches in parables

This chapter provides an excellent example of Jesus the teacher of men, and Mark the theologian of the church. We must examine the contribution of each separately and then see how they both agree in their basic insight and message.

The parable was a fairly common form of exposition in the rabbinical circles of Jesus' day, and the fact that he too adopts such a form shows how much a man of his time Jesus was, speaking the language of his people. A parable is usually distinguished from allegory by the fact that it is a story with a single point, whereas the latter gives a quite independent and separate meaning to individual items within the image or story used. In a parable the emphasis is on the real life situation and the challenge is to discover the applied meaning, whereas this latter takes precedence in the allegory to such an extent that when decoded we may not get a true-to-life picture at all (see the allegory of the wild olive, relating to reception of gentiles into the people of God, Rom 11:17–24, and the curious type of horticulture it presupposes). The parables of Jesus are all related to the kingdom that he preached, its nature, its demands, its acceptance or rejection and the like. They all breathe the atmosphere of contemporary Palestine and everyday events as they were lived and experienced. The sower sowing, the ripening harvest, the marriage feast, the fisherman at work, the woman baking, all speak immediately and directly of the kingdom as preached by Jesus. The resemblance is not something vague or external, and it is not a question of a mere metaphor but rather an affirmation that with Jesus the kingdom is as near and as all-embracing as these everyday things.

The growth parables are a particular category within the broader class of parables of the kingdom, since all of them have a common point of contrast, the organic development between the first sowing of the seed and the final harvest or end product. In this chapter we find three such parables, the sower (4:2–9), the seed growing secretly (4:26–29) and the mustard seed (4:30–32) all of them with minor variations of the same general theme. In all probability the three originally formed part of a larger collection which would naturally have been made on the basis of a common theme. The point of the parable of the sower might appear to be concentrated in the varying yields of the different types of soil at the conclusion, or the fate of the seed falling on different kinds of ground, a point that is taken up in the subsequent explanation. However, a closer look at the parable itself without the explanation shows that the real contrast is between the original sowing and the final harvest of 4:8. Despite all the various difficulties, and the frustrations the labourer is likely to have to deal with, the seed has been sown and the rich harvest is assured. One can imagine Jesus addressing such a message to his followers who were actively engaged in the ministry with him and who, we saw, did not fully understand the nature of the kingdom he preached. Their disappointment at the failure of the kingdom to manifest itself as expected can only be met by trying to explain the true nature of the kingdom and its presence in the world through the hiddenness of Jesus' ministry. His co-workers are not to be despondent, the sowing has taken place and inevitably the harvest will come. However unrelated the present activity of Jesus appears to be to the future kingdom of glory, there is a real organic growth. So take heart; for the present one must have confidence in the word of Jesus. One must go on sowing the seed, aware that in the end the harvest will come.

The other two growth parables develop slightly different aspects of this central theme. The parable of the seed growing secretly again contrasts the rich harvest with the initial sowing. It stresses the fact that once sown the earth 'of itself' produces the growth, 'he knows not how'. Here the point seems to be that man must be patient since there is really nothing he can do to hasten the harvest. Once the sowing has been done and preparations made the rest is in God's hand; 'the mills of God grind slowly' to change the metaphor slightly. One could conjecture that this parable was addressed to over-enthusiastic followers of Jesus, who because of a false concept of the kingdom felt that they could bring it on. Perhaps the Zealots, the party of political agitators, was involved since

we see traces elsewhere of a desire for Jesus to adopt the
role of political liberator (Mk 6:45; 12:14 f; Jn 6:15).
In the parable of the mustard seed the emphasis is on the
smallness of the beginnings in contrast with the full
growth, 'the greatest of all shrubs' which gives protection
and shelter. The message is clearly one of encouragement
for those who are disillusioned by the insignificance of
Jesus and his appearance, in comparison with what was
expected. They are not to be put off by what they see—
the reality is much different and much greater. John's
gospel has a saying of Jesus very similar in tone and content to this parable but stressing the idea that the grain
must *die* in order to bring fruit—but if it does it produces
'much fruit' (Jn 12:24). The paradox of small beginnings
and rich harvest has been pushed further here to explain
the scandal of death as the supreme breakthrough of
God's kingdom.

All these growth parables clearly belong to Jesus'
answer to those of his own followers who were discour-
aged by the absence of sudden and startling results from
their ministry and that of Jesus. His reply shows how
deeply he himself trusted in God and left the future in
God's hands. Yet his assurance was based on the fact that
the future was not something vague or remote, but was
rather the future of the present he now knew and experienced. They are a reminder to all would-be reformers
that in the end they must wait for God's kingdom because
if it depended on their human efforts it would be man's
doing, not God's gift. As we saw, the kingdom is first of
all the pearl of great price. This doesn't mean that the
follower of Jesus has to be passive about it; he must go
about his work recognising the hidden yet ever-present
reality of grace that meets him in his everyday existence.
His achievements of love, brotherhood and concern are

not to be abandoned or regarded as unimportant. They will always be recognised as manifestations of the kingdom and its grace, yet in the end pale reflections of the full reality 'when God will be everything to everyone' (1 Cor 15:28).

1. What is the message of the growth parables for christian faith today?

2. Write a contemporary parable making the same point.

3. Explain the relation between the kingdom of God and human endeavour in the world, especially political action.

Mk 4:10, 13–20. The explanation of the parable of the sower

At a very early stage, it would seem, the apostolic preachers and teachers applied the words and sayings of Jesus to their own situation and that of the believers. They remembered that Jesus had promised to be with them all days (Mt 28:18) that he would still be their only teacher (Mt 23:9) and that he would send his Spirit of Truth to instruct them fully and teach them all truth, since he had yet 'many things to say to them' that they could not hear at that moment (Jn 14:16 f; 16:12 f). Consequently, they felt free to put on the lips of Jesus ideas which they believed were already implicit in his words. Indeed it was their duty as 'ministers of the word' to apply his sayings to the needs of the church in the world. It is against this background that we should try to understand the explanation of the parable of the sower, which is really an exhortation based on the different yields from the various kinds of soil. This, we saw, wasn't the main contrast in the story originally but the possibility of failure was recognised in the various kinds of soil and even the varied yield from the good ground. The early church used it as a basis for an examination of conscience for believers on how in fact they had responded to the word of God which they had received. One finds the language of this instruction appearing repeatedly in the moral sections of Paul's epistles. Such phrases as 'keeping the word', 'receiving it with joy', 'the word bringing forth fruit' etc can all be paralleled in Paul as descriptions for the way in which his preaching had been received, and they belong to the exhortatory language of the Greek-speaking church, rather than to the Aramaic eschatological expression of Jesus. Indeed the explanation does not fit the original parable very well, for the whole idea of the harvest has been dropped, and the seed of the story is made to stand both for the word and those who receive the word.

Of course this does not mean that this section is unimportant or not inspired, but it does help us to understand its message better. The message is simple and straightforward, and as we shall presently see fits in admirably with the instruction Mark wishes to impart to the disciples in this chapter. As it stands it is an instruction on the right dispositions for receiving the word. The word that is received is almost a personal reality, which one must receive and accept and allow to take root. Persecution can arise because of the word, and of course Satan is its great opponent who seeks to snatch it from the heart immediately it has been sown. All this is in line with Mark's own understanding of the gospel, which can be identified with Jesus, and a man can lose his life or leave all for the sake of Jesus or the gospel (8:35; 10:29). And as we have seen, since Satan is the great enemy of Jesus, those who are to be sent to preach must also be endowed with power over Satan if their ministry is to be as effective as that of Jesus.

1. Describe in contemporary terms the four different attitudes relating to the word that are mentioned in this passage.

2. Why were the early christians entitled to interpret the words of Jesus in this way?

Mk 4:21-34. Mark's contribution

Mark had this body of material available to him as well as a number of other scattered sayings of Jesus, 4:11 f, 4:21-25. To these he added or reshaped the introduction 4:1 f, and the conclusion 4:33 f, to give a fully rounded discourse on parables that was in line with his own particular theological ideas, especially that of the disciples as those chosen to be with Jesus in order to receive the mystery of the kingdom which is being entrusted to them.

To begin with it is important to distinguish the two different audiences in this chapter and their two different places of meeting with Jesus. Verse 1f shows the large enthusiastic crowd that Jesus always seemed capable of drawing to himself, but the boat which had been provided earlier 'lest the crowd crush him' but not actually used then (3:9) is now brought into play. Jesus thereby withdraws somewhat from the crowd, but this is merely an indication of a much more serious spiritual separation being caused by his words which the crowds at large cannot understand. This separation expresses itself more clearly at 4:10-12 where two groups have emerged, 'those around him with the twelve' and 'those outside'. This latter term is not just an indication of location but a determination of a certain attitude to Jesus (see 3:31) which Mark now explains more precisely. The inner circle, always for Mark centred on the twelve, have the mystery of the kingdom given to them. The use of the singular here, as distinct from mysteries (plural) in Matthew and Luke, indicates that he has a very central idea in mind, which in the light of his whole theology can only mean a correct understanding of the person of Jesus. There is a mystery of divine grace and election in all this, for faith is a gift of God, and Jesus chose 'whom he would himself' (3:13). On the other hand for those outside everything appears as one huge riddle or enigma. There is a conscious play on the word 'parable' here, which in both Greek and Aramaic can have the twofold meaning of story or riddle. It is not a question of Jesus using parables in order to obscure the truth he wishes to communicate. Rather the fact is that for those who do not 'have the eyes to see or the ears to hear', as the prophet Isaiah put it about his own generation, what is in itself perfectly simple and straightforward turns out to be the very opposite. Scripture, especially the prophets, can often be so astounded at the failure of Israel to grasp the reality of God's presence in her midst that it will make it appear as though God caused their blindness as a judgment against them, when in fact God yearns for their repentance. So it is with Jesus and his generation.

The disciples however must not think that because they have been specially favoured they can ignore God's challenge to them to open their hearts. Mark takes up the explanation of the parable of the sower, a question and explanation which now suits his purpose admirably and which he uses to goad his readers to a greater sense of purpose in trying to understand what they hear. Furthermore he adds the series of other sayings of Jesus (4:21–25) all related to the theme of generosity in hearing the word.

First of all the purpose for entrusting the mystery to them is not to set them apart as an élitist group with no care for those outside. Rather the mystery (4:11) is hidden with them now (4:22) precisely in order to be brought to light later. In the meantime they must dedicate themselves totally to hearing, because their understanding will be proportionately related to such dedication.

All this took place within the house, but the conclusion (4:33 f) makes it clear that Mark envisages the action as having moved outside again, for there the distinction is drawn between teaching in parables to the crowds and special instruction apart for his own disciples. Presumably, then, we are to see the movement outside starting at 4:26 for the two growth parables we have already discussed. Both of them deal with the hiddenness of the kingdom and its present obscurity, and so they relate directly to the theme of the blindness of people of which the evangelist is treating. Like the master-artist that he is Mark has chosen, from all the varied parables of Jesus that we find in the other two gospels, only the growth parables which suit his purpose so well. The problem of faith and unbelief was a problem for Jesus' original followers, for Mark's readers and for us today within the church. What is it that distinguishes those who believe from those outside for whom everything is a riddle? Mark does not try to reduce the problem or judge the motives but he is acutely aware of the fact. In the end, he feels, it is a question of meaning—the pieces fall together and the hidden, obscure everyday things of life turn out to be the language of God's secret presence in our midst. Those to whom the gift is given of seeing things in this way must realise that this is a gift, and recognise their responsibilities to those outside. But the gift is also a challenge, as the subsequent drama of the disciples will show. Indeed several scenes from now they will be asked whether they too have eyes and do not see and ears and do not hear (8:14). A gift is never just a gift, if it comes from God and concerns a basic understanding of human existence and the ultimate destiny of man.

1. How best can those to whom the mystery is given communicate with those outside?

2. Explain how generosity in trying to understand the mystery can bring a deeper understanding of one's faith.

3. How does Mark's treatment of the problem of belief and unbelief help you to explain this problem in our world?

Mk 4:35–5:43. The mighty deeds of Jesus

(i) *4:35–41. The stilling of the storm.* Eventually the little boat sets out on its first journey, even though it had been prepared as far back as 3:9 at the request of Jesus 'lest he be crushed by the crowd'. It was used subsequently at 4:1 to give his instruction in parables which, we have seen, separated the true believers from those outside and it now carries the chosen ones in the company of other boats. A storm was seen in the old testament as a particular manifestation of God's power and majesty and man's helplessness, and yet the deep was a place where evil monsters dwelt. One gets the impression that Mark is here describing a particularly dangerous situation for the christian communities of his own day, symbolised by the boats being tossed in the waves. Like the travellers described in Ps 107:23–32 the christians should cry to the Lord in their distress, for 'he made the storm be still, and the waves of the sea were hushed and he brought them to their desired haven'. Yahweh is Lord of the storm, and can use it as his instrument of judgement or command it to cease as though it were an evil power under his control. Jesus is asleep, a christian euphemism for death, and so this colourful detail may well refer to the absence occasioned by his death and the delay in returning to save his own who are tossed by the seas of persecution and trouble that is the Roman Empire.

Against this old testament background and church situation we can appreciate the lesson in faith the story is meant to teach and how well it fits into Mark's account. The disciples are terrified in the midst of the storm and it does not occur to them to pray even in old testament categories. Rather they cry out helplessly and chidingly to Jesus: 'Teacher do you not care if we perish?' There is no great christological content or deep expression of faith in such a plea, by contrast with Matthew's 'Lord save us we are perishing' on the same occasion (Mt 8:25). Jesus performs his mighty deed, rebuking the sea as though it were possessed by an evil spirit, thereby illustrating that he shares the cosmic power that belonged to Yahweh, Lord of the storm. Jesus is obviously highly dissatisfied with their attitude: 'Have you no faith yet?' Their previous election and instruction has left them unchanged, and even now their reaction is characteristically feeble. They 'feared greatly', a sure sign that faith is still lacking and their only response to this display of power is to ask the right question 'Who is this that the wind and sea obey him?' The answer should have been obvious but for them at least it was not. Mark's readers must be on their guard against similar disillusionment even if for the present Jesus appears to sleep and they are tossed about. Have courage, 'he is risen', is the message they must eventually get from this gospel.

1. How does the message of this story for first-century christians apply to the church situation today?

2. What do you think is the significance of the other boats in this story?

(ii) *5 : 1–20. The cure of the Gerasene demoniac.* This exorcism story serves Mark with another example of Jesus' victory over Satan. There are many embellishments in the narrative which may well have belonged to it before the evangelist took it over, but they have certainly served his overall presentation well. The terrible condition of the demoniac and his strength by comparison with any human agent are highlighted in 5 : 3–6. The request of the demons to enter the swine and their subsequent flight into the sea link this story with previous episodes. The depths of the sea was the place where evil spirits lived according to popular mythology, and the fact that Jesus could control the turbulence of the deep is now further illustrated by his power over the evil spirits in allowing them to return to their own place. The fact that their name is Legion helps to underline Jesus' reply to the scribes that he is opposed to the whole realm of Satan and is in no way in league with any of his underlings.

The nucleus of the story shows Satan and Jesus confronting each other in typical fashion. The demons use exorcism language, 'I adjure you by God do not torment me' (5 : 7) and show a correct knowledge of Jesus' name as at 1 : 24 and 3 : 11, but this does not in any way derogate from the authority and power of Jesus. The outcome is inevitable for the possessed man is restored to his right mind and sits at the feet of Jesus. He wishes to be 'with Jesus', that is become a disciple (3 : 14), but this particular request is refused for Jesus calls 'whom he would himself'. The man is told to return and tell his own people what

things *the Lord* (that is 'God', see Lk 8:39), has done for
him (5:19). Instead the man went and told them of Jesus
because he has been able to see the clear identity between
him and the Lord, something that the disciples have not
yet seen (5:20). There is an echo of the missionary activity of the church in this verse and we might be tempted
to ask why Mark does not have Jesus enjoin silence at this
point. It would seem that he sees in the episode some
anticipation of the christian mission even though as yet
these pagan people are not prepared to receive Jesus, pre-
ferring the tyranny of Satan to the liberating presence of
this strange miracle worker. There is no need to call for
secrecy because there is no enthusiastic acceptance of
Jesus by the crowd and no false proclamation of him by
the man once he has been restored to his right mind. The
seeds of the future mission can thus be allowed to be
sown.

*1. Explain the reaction of the people, the request of the
cured man and the refusal of Jesus in the light of the
contemporary church situation.*

*2. Contrast this episode with the previous one, and the
Beelzebub controversy (3:20–35).*

(iii) *Two miraculous cures.* Two miraculous cures of
people in extreme physical conditions (5:23 and 26) help
to underline the power of Jesus to save (5:34) and to
raise from the dead (5:41) provided the proper dispositions of faith are present. There appears to be a conscious
contrast between the ruler and the woman on the one hand
and the disciples and those who came from the ruler's
house on the other. The former have an unquestioning
confidence in Jesus' power whereas the latter are preoc-
cupied about externals, the thronging crowd and not

troubling the master further. As always in Mark the crowd merely form the backdrop to the scene and play no active part in the events. Yet Mark does not wish to exclude them positively from the presence of Jesus, and whenever somebody shows the right kind of attitude to him he is willing to give his healing touch. Thus the woman in the crowd must meet Jesus face to face before the saving word is addressed to her. Curiously, only three of the disciples are taken along to witness the second miracle, together with the parents of the child. The same three disciples share in the transfiguration and agony scenes (9:2; 14:33) and presumably their presence now is to prepare them for those important experiences. The ecstatic amazement of the bystanders classifies the incident as a theophany, but the command to silence, however improbable it may be historically, shows that for Mark's reader this incident cannot yet be understood fully without reference to Jesus' own victory over death which discloses fully the true source of his power.

1. What is to be learned about the nature of true faith from this episode?

2. Where today are individual believers addressed personally by Christ?

Mk 6:1–6. Conclusion: rejection of Jesus at Nazareth

This second scene of the first act which has been characterised by the gradual separation of Jesus' true disciples from others, including his own, is now brought to a conclusion with his rejection by the people of Nazareth. It is clearly intended as Mark's answer to a perennial question for the early church, 'How did the Jews fail to recognise their messiah?' (cf Rom 9–11). As earlier at 3:20 f in the case of his relations, they judge Jesus merely by the externals of his life and find his common origin with them a stumbling block to true faith. They are prepared to concede a special quality to this teaching and activity but this does not lead them any nearer to faith in him, but rather 'they took offence at him', that is they found his origins among the common people a real obstacle to belief, for they still clung to ideas of the glorious, other-world messiah. Jesus' reaction clearly links this scene with the previous attitude of 'his own' and shows how necessary it was for him 'to choose whom he would himself' as the basis for his community, no matter how slow they are to come to full faith in him. The general lack of faith prevents Jesus from performing any miracle there, since one must presume some basic goodwill and openness as a prelude to God's visitation of his people. Yet here, as elsewhere, there are individuals in the midst of so much unbelief who can receive a personal favour from him since he knows the inner dispositions of each individually.

The section is of particular interest because of the background information it gives about Jesus' family and early life at Nazareth. Much is sometimes made of the mention here of 'the brothers of Jesus' (see 3:31 also) and in general protestant scholars would tend to see them as Jesus' full blood brothers, whereas catholics, accepting the perpetual virginity of our Lady, give the phrase a wider connotation referring to his relations within the oriental notions of family kinship. There is plenty of old testament evidence for this wider use of the term 'brother' and considering that two of Jesus' brothers mentioned here, James and Joses, are elsewhere said to be sons of another Mary (15:40) it appears the more likely interpretation. And this woman is probably to be identified with Mary the wife of Clopas, 'the sister' of Jesus' mother who stood with her at the cross (Jn 19:25).

 1. *How do you explain the failure of the people of Nazareth to accept Jesus?*
 2. *What was the significance for Mark of this passage and the presentation of Jesus that it gives?*
 3. *What have you learned about Jesus' childhood and 'hidden life' from this passage?*

4

Scene three: Jesus and the disciples
Mk 6:6–8:30

This scene leading up to Peter's confession at 8:29 is usually described as 'the bread section' because there seems to be a deliberate concentration on the theme of bread throughout: 6:34–44, 52; 7:28; 8:1–10, 14–21. The section can be compared with the 'bread of life' discourse in John (chapter 6) which begins with a feeding miracle and concludes with Peter's declaration, 'Lord to whom shall we go? You have the words of eternal life' (Jn 6:68). The understanding of Jesus as the bread of life has led to the separation of the true disciples from those who went back and walked no more with him. This seems to be Mark's overall intention also even though he is working with traditional material that cannot be welded into a unified whole as easily as in John. Though he seems to direct all the attention to the little group who have been specially chosen and to whom the mystery of the kingdom has been granted, Mark does not entirely exclude the wider audience no matter how little they are able to comprehend the person to whom they feel attracted. The true christian community must never be insensitive to the needs of the crowd, for it is called into existence in order to serve those needs, as this section will show.

Mk 6:6–30. Mission of the twelve and the death of the Baptist

The section opens with a simple statement that Jesus went around the villages teaching, but this merely serves as an introduction to the mission of the twelve, which must always be set in the context of the mission and activity of Jesus. At the same time the terms of their commissioning (6:7) and the subsequent report of their activity (6:13) show that for Mark at least this particular tour of Galilee is provisional and preparatory. Both Matthew and Luke present the disciples proclaiming the kingdom of God at this point, but Mark is careful to avoid such a statement. In his presentation they have not yet understood the mystery concerning the kingdom that is entrusted to them, nor could they, as we shall see from Act 2; so they can only engage in preaching that 'men should do penance', which was the Baptist's function (1:4), and in casting out demons who are opposed to the good news of the gospel (4:15). The actual instructions for their tour appear strange to the modern reader, and this was equally true for Mark's Roman readers. They apply to the Palestinian scene where wandering teachers were common, and the urgency of their message can be detected from the fact that they are not to delay to pass everyday greetings and they are to travel light (cf Mt 10:23). 'Casting off the dust of their feet' as a testimony against those who refuse to hear them should be seen as a gesture of defiance that is tantamount to declaring prophetic judgement against them as unbelievers. These instructions help us to catch something of the atmosphere of extreme urgency and finality that marked the original preaching of Jesus. In all probability Mark has preserved them now for his readers so that they might retain this same sense of immediacy and crisis in their lives as a result of their christian vocation. Whereas Mark is quite reticent in relating the original commission of the twelve, he is much more generous in reporting their return. For the only time in his gospel they are called apostles, and they report to Jesus all that they 'have done and taught', a typical expression for the ministry of Jesus as a whole (cf Acts 1:1). However provisional Mark considers this trip to have been it still served him as the starting point of the later apostolic mission of the church which the risen Lord will entrust to his representatives.

The death of the Baptist, told with all the art of a popular story teller, serves to fill the dramatic pause between the departure and return of the twelve. They were appointed 'to be with Jesus' and so nothing can take place in their absence. For Mark this death serves as an indication of the fate the fearless preacher of the gospel can expect from civil authority at a time when Nero's persecution is beginning to threaten christians. At 1:2 Mark has implicitly identified John with Elijah by describing him as the messenger who was expected to usher in the messianic times which the prophet Malachi speaks of (Mal 3:1). According to 2 Kgs 2:11 Elijah did not die but was taken up to heaven in a whirlwind and so he was expected to return to announce the arrival of the messiah at the end of the age (Mal 4:5). Mark identifies the fate of the Baptist as the expected Elijah with that of the Son of Man at 9:11 ff, and so this description of his death serves to prepare for the suffering role of the messiah to be disclosed in the second act of the drama.

1. How far is apostolic endeavour dependent on a true understanding of Jesus?

2. What is the lesson for christians today from the fate of the Baptist?

Mk 6:31–44. Retreat to the desert and first feeding miracle

The scene for this miracle is the desert; and for those acquainted with the story of the exodus it had immediate associations with the manna or bread from heaven with which Yahweh fed his people during their wandering in the wilderness. In Mark's account the retreat to the desert was intended to be a rest for the disciples, lately abroad as apostles. The crowd is enthusiastic and willing, and Mark shows Jesus' compassion for them despite the fact that they do not belong to those to whom the mystery is given. Mark always describes the larger following of Jesus as 'the crowd' (singular) almost like the chorus in a Greek tragedy. They are never hostile but their external attraction and lack of any real comprehension are highlighted. They are excited about the teaching of Jesus and bring along the sick (1 : 28, 33); they come to Jesus (2 : 13; 3 : 20), they follow him (12 : 15; 3 : 7; 10 : 32); they gather around (5 : 21; 10 : 1). They press around Jesus (3 : 9; 5 : 24, 31) and prevent him from eating (3 : 21; 6 : 31) or obstruct him in his contact with individuals (2 : 4; 5 : 21). Yet despite all this external enthusiasm their response is feeble: 'he does all things well' (7 : 27) or 'we never saw the like' (2 : 12). Thus they could never serve Jesus as those to whom the mystery of his own ministry might be entrusted, and so his disciples are separated from them (4 : 10). At the same time they are not to be rejected or despised, as the attitude of Jesus makes clear both here and at 7 : 14. The separation between the community of disciples and the crowd is not absolute but rather both have different levels of relationship with Jesus, and the former must never consider themselves as an élite or superior group, 'for nothing is hidden except to be made manifest' (4 : 22).

As told here the feeding story has two terms of reference. On the one hand the abundance of the food and the satisfaction of the participants recalls the banquet which was such a popular description of the joy and plenty of messianic times. At the same time the action of Jesus in regard to bread, 'he took the loaves, blessed and broke and gave them to his disciples', is a very clear echo of his action at the last supper (Mk 14:22). For Mark's readers, therefore, the story should recall for them the meaning of the Lord's supper which they were privileged to celebrate and it was a foretaste of the messianic banquet which they would soon partake of to the full. Others see further symbolism in the *twelve* baskets of fragments taken up as representing the twelve tribes of Israel, and a fish was a popular symbol for Jesus in the early church, as can be seen from various early mosaics and drawings.

1. What should be the attitude of the christian community to the crowds?

2. Does this story help you to understand the meaning of the eucharist more fully?

Mk 6:45–51. Jesus' walking on the waters

The way in which Mark describes the dismissal of the crowd indicates that Jesus is anything but pleased with the overall reaction. He has to compel the disciples to enter the boat as though further contact with the crowd would not be proper, and he himself dismisses the crowd. It may well be that these rather strong expressions are an indication of certain messianic feelings that John describes as 'wanting to take him by force and make him king' (Jn 6:15). This conclusion is supported by the fact that Jesus goes alone to pray, as after the first day of the ministry when he was clearly dissatisfied with the reaction of Simon and those who were with him (Mk 1:35–39). Unlike Luke's account, where Jesus prays on many different occasions, Mark reserves the prayer of Jesus for three moments of apparent failure of his mission (14:34 ff, the agony scene, is the third instance). That evening Jesus appears to his disciples 'walking on the waters', a theophany-like apparition that again portrays him as lord of the sea. However, not even this is sufficient for the disciples. Their reaction is one of fear which Mark wants to highlight: 'they were utterly astounded' when Jesus joins them in the boat, we are told. His concluding remark is a comment full of significance on the whole episode. The disciples' reaction is based on their failure to understand Jesus as the giver of bread, and this results from their sharing the attitude of the religious and political leaders : 'their hearts were hardened' (cf 3:5). This is a scathing comment on their failure to comprehend Jesus or his goodness, and the evangelist clearly wants to underline the utter seriousness of their position, despite their special election.

1. Why did Jesus refuse to accept the role of political liberator which would have made him more easily acceptable to the Jews?

2. What is the role of the christian community in politics?

Mk 6:52–56; 7:1–23. The things that defile

A brief summary of Jesus' healing ministry among pagans serves Mark as an introduction to what is to follow—the generous goodness of Jesus is a striking contrast to the selfish exclusivism that is to be described in detail in chapter 7. This summary, like others in the gospel earlier, serves to show that Jesus was untiring in his care for the lowly. Surprisingly on this occasion there is no command to silence however. Yet the reason for it still operates, for the dangers of misunderstanding Jesus are still very live.

Originally law had its proper setting within the covenant context where it was an expression of the will of the covenant God who had generously intervened to choose Israel as his own people (Ex 19–24). Thus the *torah* was seen as God's gift to his people, and there was never any quesion of making its binding force so absolute that it became a heavy and insupportable burden. In the course of the centuries, however, this had changed drastically. The law was divorced from its covenant setting and given an absolute value of its own. During the exile and post-exilic period (from 580 BC on) it served to separate the Jews from their neighbours since they were then deprived of independent civil status. The rabbinical schools took on a special importance for there the law was interpreted and applied to everyday situations and circumstances, thereby giving rise to the tradition of the ancients, the oral additions that had grown up around the *torah*. At the time of Christ there were 613 different prescriptions in all, moral, cultic and ritual, all equally binding and of the same gravity. Unfortunately this excessive emphasis on the law, something that was good in itself, had made mere external observance the supreme test of goodness, to the neglect of basic duties to one's fellow man, as we have seen earlier in regard to the sabbath law.

In this instance the Pharisees were annoyed because Jesus' disciples did not observe the traditions of the elders, so dear to them. Jesus replied by selecting a particularly striking example of Jewish tradition which when observed to the letter made it impossible to observe the fourth command of the decalogue: 'honour your father and your mother'. According to the Jewish tradition if one made a solemn oath to God it could not be violated no matter what the circumstance. In this instance, it would seem, people were dedicating to God under oath what should have gone to the support of their parents and then claiming immunity from the clear command of God to support one's father and mother. This was a flagrant example of legalism gone wild, and a rejection of all that God's law stood for. 'And many such things you do'. Jesus has shown the absurdity of their attitude.

Afterwards Jesus explains his whole approach to such matters in a positive way for the people first, and then subsequently for the disciples in a further elaboration. His first explanation was 'a parable' and so not clear to the people and in need of further elucidation for the disciples themselves 'in the house'. What defiles a man is from within, not those things which according to Jewish ritual law are 'unclean' because of their profane use, so that contact with them makes one ritually impure. This seems an obvious and straightforward position for us, but for those who identified ritual with moral law it was a startling innovation. At one stroke Jesus dismisses as unnecessary the whole elaborate paraphernalia of Jewish ritual, 'declaring all foods clean'. It is the heart of man that is important, not external appearances, and it is this that determines one's true religious attitude. This instruction given specially to the disciples is an important clue to their failure to appreciate or understand Jesus and his mission. It is equally important for Mark's readers, non-Jews as they were, to realise that being followers of Jesus did not mean observing the Jewish law as well, something over-zealous Jewish christians were demanding, as is clear from Paul's disputes in his epistles to the Galatians and Romans.

1. Why has legalism no place in christian morality?

2. Where in the church today would one find the attitude condemned by Jesus?

Mk 7:24–37; 8:1–10. A tour among the gentiles

The judgement of Jesus on the closed religious attitudes of the Jews must have been a welcome relief to Mark's Roman readers. However, Mark feels it necessary to portray Jesus at work outside Palestine, Tyre and Sidon (7 : 24) and Decapolis (7 : 31), to assure them that the barriers between Jew and Greek have indeed been broken down. Peter's action in receiving Cornelius and his household into the church (Acts 10) had to be justified more than once subsequently to over-zealous Jewish christian converts. No doubt this attitude prevailed in Rome also since Paul first addressed himself to Jews when he arrived in the city (Acts 28), and presumably there were christian converts among them. This tour of Jesus outside Palestine is therefore highly significant. The Greek woman of Syrophoenician origin who asks him to heal his daughter puts the whole problem in focus. At first Jesus would appear to be ungracious towards her request though probably nothing disrespectful is intended by describing the gentiles as dogs (the Greek word used is a diminutive, which may be intended to soften the apparent harshness). Jesus puts the typical Jewish case: the blessings of the kingdom belong to the children of the kingdom. The woman recognises that in a certain sense this is true; it is a case of Jews first then the Greeks in the divine plan. But this request to share in the good things of the master's table is not meant to question that divine order or to diminish the gift to the Jews, but only a plea to be allowed to participate to some limited degree in God's goodness. There is no question of refusing the request. Indeed the second feeding miracle that is reported without any real change of audience or location (8:1–10) indicates that it is not merely a question of gentiles being allowed to gather the crumbs, for the disciples are to give them of the abundance of the table so that they too can be satisfied (8:8).

In between these two episodes there is a further account of Jesus' healing activity in foreign parts. On this occasion, however, Mark prefers to give an individual instance of his kindness. Jesus takes the deaf man aside privately, away from the crowd, and cures him. Mark describes the effect of Jesus' action by saying that 'his hearing' (literally, not 'ears') was opened and 'the chain of his tongue' was loosed, and from finding it difficult to speak previously (7:32) he was now able 'to speak plainly'. This episode is missing completely in Luke, and Matthew has only an account of the general healing ministry (Mt 15:29–31), but nothing about a specific cure. The details are clearly important for Mark and they, together with the story of the opening of the eyes of the blind man (8:22–26), are part of the rare use in his gospel of special material not found in the others. The fact that both episodes occur in the immediate lead-in to Peter's confession prompts the suggestion that Mark was thinking of both symbolically in terms of faith—true understanding of Jesus comes from hearing and seeing properly. Only then is the chain of the tongue loosened, that is, the demonic enslavement that makes it impossible either to receive the gospel oneself or proclaim it to others is broken.

The performance of the miracle in private and the subsequent command for silence is by now a familiar trait of Mark's presentation (1:43 f; 5:43; 8:23, 26). Again it fails to bring about the required effect and the reaction is as usual enthusiastic and generous. The making of 'the deaf to hear and the dumb to speak' was expected of the messiah according to Is 35:5–6, and Mark may want to indicate that these foreigners are as near to understanding the truth about Jesus as are the specially chosen disciples. Though the command to silence is ineffective, and though there is no displeasure at its failure, it is a warning for Mark's reader that the full truth about Jesus is still veiled and that there must be no hasty acceptance of him as a mere miracle worker.

1. What does this section tell us about the missionary task of the church today?

2. Explain fully the details of this cure in terms of christian faith.

3. What does the command to silence at this point have to say for the modern reader of Mark's gospel?

Mk 8:11–13. Refusal to give a sign

The previous section has shown that faith is in the end the gift of God, requiring the healing hand of Jesus to touch our human weakness if we are to understand properly. Yet this very human weakness will in its pride always seek to understand by itself and this is the mentality that is portrayed in the Pharisees' request for a sign from heaven. Mark suggests that this request is a temptation for Jesus, and later we learn that the performance of signs and wonders that could deceive even the elect is a mark of the false Christs of the end-time (Mk 13:22). To ask for a sign from heaven is to expect God to condescend to human pride and reason, and such an attitude could never lead to true faith. Faith begins with man's acceptance of his need for God, and thus he is moved to go out of himself and start on the journey that leads to

God. Jesus refuses to toy with their human attitudes, and utters a cry of despair against 'this generation', a term that with the prophets has a special reference to human stubbornness and infidelity. Once again the boat serves as a means to separate himself from such worldly temptations.

1. Why is the attitude that seeks a sign from heaven so opposed to true faith?

2. How was Jesus tempted by this request?

3. Where in the church today does one find a similar attitude?

Mk 8:14–21. The discourse concerning the bread

The significance of Mark's concentration on bread now emerges clearly because this brief discourse draws out the full implications of the feeding miracles for the disciples' faith in Jesus. At 6:52 their fear at the theophany of Jesus was the direct result of their failure to understand concerning the loaves and this failure was attributed to their hardness of heart. A certain development has taken place in the interval, because instead of passing judgement the evangelist has Jesus question them in regard to their dispositions with a mounting series of swift, sharp questions so as to bring them back over the previous feeding miracles, climaxing with the plea: 'Do you not yet understand?' The queries 'Are your hearts still *hardened*?' and 'Having eyes do you not *see* and ears do you not *hear*?' now put to the disciples in form of a question the very words of judgement that have already been addressed to the religious and civil leaders (3:5) and those outside (4:10 f). Besides, the miracle which preceded (cure of a deaf-and-dumb man) and the one that follows (cure of a blind man) are given their full significance in relation to the genesis of the disciples' faith.

The cross-questioning arises from what appears to be a very ordinary omission on the part of the disciples—they forget to bring bread with them for the boat trip, having only one loaf with them (8:14). Verse 15, a caution of Jesus concerning the leaven of the Pharisees and of Herod, would seem to interrupt the flow of the narrative because 8:16 could follow quite naturally after 8:14: 'And they discussed it with one another, saying "We have no bread".' One might have imagined that they would have remembered the two feeding miracles and the abundance of fragments left over at this point. Even the one loaf that they do have could have served as the basis for a further feeding miracle. Yet they are so unthinking and so totally blind to the meaning of Christ's presence that such a request never crosses their mind. The fact that Jesus recalls the two previous miracles for them (8:19 f) shows that Mark is being quite ironic about their utter lack of appreciation of Jesus who can provide them with bread in abundance. Indeed we might be prompted to ask whether the evangelist is alluding to Jesus personally as the bread of life who is not recognised when he says that 'they had only one loaf with them in the boat,' yet has them forget about the implications of this for their food.

This would give point to the warning to them to be on their guard against the leaven of Herod and the Pharisees (8:15) which, we said, seems to break the flow of the narrative. In Matthew's version of the same saying the leaven is that of the Pharisees and Sadducees and is explained in terms of their teaching, something the disciples understand subsequently (Mt 16:12). Mark makes no such identification, however, nor does he tell us that they understood the reference. We must infer what he has in mind from the context of his gospel and at 3:6 and 12:13 we find the same two parties, Pharisees and Herodians, conspiring together to put Jesus to death. The warning in Mark would then appear to refer to the fate that is in store for Jesus, and the shock that this will give to the disciples' acceptance of him as the Christ. In order to be the bread of life for them Jesus must first give himself on their behalf, and because their minds are closed to understanding the true meaning of his present ministry they are not even able to recognise what he has to offer them in their immediate needs. 'Do you not *yet* understand?'

1. Why did the disciples fail to understand the ministry of Jesus?

2. How should the bread miracles have helped them to this understanding and how can they help us today?

3. Compare the disciples' attitude to faith in Jesus with that of the crowd.

Mk 8:22–26. Cure of a blind man

As already indicated this miracle is closely related to the cure of the deaf-and-dumb man and the intervening discourse. Again it is one of the few pieces of independent material used by Mark and so takes on added significance in regard to his message. In the passion narrative seeing and believing are closely related in terms of understanding the meaning of Jesus' death and exaltation (14:62; 15:32, 39). Here the same combination is to be found, and the two-stage recovery of sight, so that in the end 'he saw everything clearly' is consciously intended to describe true faith and the stages of coming to full knowledge of Jesus. We have reached the turning point of the gospel, and Peter will soon make his profession of faith on behalf of the other disciples. But for Mark this is only the end of the first act, a stage on the way. There will be need for further activity by Jesus before full faith is brought about. Thus the way is opened for the second act in the very climax of the first. Once again the secrecy motif is prominent in that the man is taken aside outside the village and told not to return there after the cure. Jesus is intent on eliciting some recognition from the disciples now, and further involvement with enthusiastic well-wishers could only impede his true purpose at this point, so that privacy is particularly important. It should remind Mark's readers that easy acceptance of Jesus is not the way to apostolic faith that is able to share the full good news with others.

1. How is 'seeing' related to believing?

2. How can those who do not see in the literal sense still believe?

3. Explain the two stages of seeing in this miracle in terms of faith.

Mk 8:27–30. The confession of Peter

Simon, one of the first pair of brothers to be called, was given a new name at the election of the twelve (3:16), and though Mark does not explain the significance of this name for us as does Matthew at 16:16 f, he is clearly aware of its significance and the change of status it implied. He never once uses the double name Simon Peter as do Matthew and Luke, but always retains 'Peter' after the head of the group was so named, with one exception. At 14:37 during the agony he is asked: 'Simon are you asleep?' The disciple has reverted to his old state and is about to deny Jesus, and Mark duly indicates this temporary abandoning of discipleship. The evangelist would naturally have been keenly aware of what this new name meant to Peter, since Papias calls him Peter's interpreter,

and so he would have been anxious to convey that meaning to the reader. Here at Caesarea Philippi Peter is acting in his role as spokesman and leader of the community
of disciples, and his profession is made in the name of all
since the question is addressed to all ('you' is plural). The
question itself is highly important in terms of faith and
its meaning. Indeed this is the question of faith *par excel-
lence,* for men must be left free ultimately to decide such
a fundamental question for themselves even though, as
the opening verses of the next act make clear, the ways
of men can often be more the ways of Satan than those of
God (8:33). Jesus as Mark has presented him has never
attempted to prove his claim. All his actions have been
capable of being understood in the light of that claim
provided one has eyes to see and ears to hear.

The reply of the disciples here shows that men's reaction to Jesus have been on the whole favourable but at
the same time they have not gone far enough in their
appreciation of him or their estimation of his work. This
is true of men's reaction to Jesus in Mark's presentation
but at last the disciples have progressed farther than the
crowd: 'Thou art the Christ.' We have already seen that
this was an important title for Jesus in Mark's view, provided the way in which it applied to him was properly
understood. For the evangelist this meant that Jesus had
fulfilled the role of messiah so completely that it has become descriptive of his person; he is not Jesus the Christ,
but Jesus Christ. The disciples' reactions will soon show
that they have not yet recognised that Jesus' very person
is involved in his office, and that that will mean *losing*
himself in order to *be* himself. They have advanced in
their understanding but they are not yet ready for such a
harsh gospel. And so they must keep their insight to

themselves until it is further clarified in the light of the drama that lies ahead.

1. Explain Mark's understanding of Peter's role in the community.

2. Why is Peter's confession still inadequate?

3. When do christians share such an inadequate view of Jesus?

5

Scene one: the path of the Son of Man Mk 8:31–10:52

The second act of the drama begins immediately by showing the way the messiah must go. Mark does not wish his readers to come to an easy acceptance of Jesus as the Christ, without any appreciation of the way of the messiah. Thus the first act ended with the command to silence, since any proclamation of Jesus simply as the Christ could only lead to a total misunderstanding of him and his mission. The way leads to Jerusalem, but not to be enthroned there as David's successor. This was the most popular expectation of the messiah in Jesus' time, and it was the one that posed the greatest threat to Roman political rule in Palestine at the time of Mark's writing. But for Jesus and for Mark Jerusalem is no longer the city of the great king, but the place where God's act of salvation is to be dramatically revealed by Jesus' giving of himself as a ransom for many. It is only when this aspect of Jesus and his mission is understood and accepted by the disciple that a christian profession of faith can be made. That Peter's profession 'thou art the Christ' is not sufficient is clear from the fact that many false Christs are to be expected declaring 'I am he', and deceiving if possible even the elect (13:22). Thus if the same elect are really to appreciate him whose call they have answered,

78

they must be prepared to go beyond a merely external, humanly inspired understanding of the messiah and his mission.

To achieve such an understanding there is little that Jesus can say that will convince the disciples of this aspect of his mission. Consequently his task is to lead them to Jerusalem so that they may participate in the traumatic events that lie ahead. The fact that they will be missing at the vital moment and show themselves all too human in their reactions only helps to underline the similar problems and reactions of Mark's readers in Nero's persecution, when christians were used as the scapegoat for the troubles of a corrupt imperial administration. However, the darkest hour is before the dawn, and the disciples of Jesus may waver at the moment of crisis, but they are prepared to hear the final word of the gospel and act accordingly. 'Jesus is risen and will go before you to Galilee . . . there you will see him, as he told you' (Mk 16:7 f). This is the way ahead that we must now explore in detail.

We can distinguish three different stages of this journey. The first phase runs from 8:31–10:52 and is built around the threefold prediction of the passion at 8:31 ff, 9:30 ff and 10:32 ff. All three are given as the group journey through Galilee on the way to Jerusalem and are interspersed with instruction on the nature of discipleship. The second phase takes place in Jerusalem itself 11:1–13:37. Jesus passes judgement on the city in word and action and then engages in controversies with the religious leaders which are parallel to those at 2:1–3: 6. This phase is concluded with the apocalyptic discourse which tells of the future victory of the Son of Man despite his apparent failure. Thirdly, the account of the passion and resurrection, 14:1–16:8, brings to completion the

story of Jesus and the call of the disciples. Here the revelation of Jesus is completed in and through his fulfilment
of his vocation as the well beloved son.

Mk 8:31–38. First prediction of the passion

Jesus and Peter are the two central figures here, just as
they were in the concluding episode of the previous act,
but there is a marked contrast between the two scenes.
To begin with Jesus does not speak of himself directly
but refers rather to the Son of Man, a figure who had only
appeared twice previously in the gospel (2:28; 3:5), in
references that spoke of his heavenly authority over sin
and the sabbath.

Peter's role too has changed: the spokesman for a
group of groping disciples trying to understand, has become the agent of Satan obstructing the true way of God's
ambassador. The tension between Satan and Jesus has
been a recurring theme in act one ever since the original
meeting between the two adversaries in the desert. Now,
however, Satan's opposition is of a more subtle kind, trying to influence the course of Jesus' ministry by what
appears to be an eminently reasonable suggestion.
Furthermore, we are no longer on the road to Caesarea
Philippi, alone with the little group of disciples. The
crowd is called together as well as the disciples for the
instruction since it has universal significance.

The Son of Man title probably had its origins in the
apocalyptic Book of Daniel, a form of literature which,
we saw, flourished in late judaism, with the object of
consoling those who were suffering for their faith; God
would soon intervene in a striking and decisive way to
destroy the powers of evil and vindicate his elect. In the
book of Daniel 'one like a son of man' is a glorious other-

worldly figure who has special access to the Ancient of
Days and is invested with power, dignity and honour
(Dan 7:13). Here, however, he is a lowly suffering figure,
at least in the present, but in the end his true dignity will
be revealed as judge of mankind (8:38). Though scho-
larly opinion is divided on the point, in all probability
Jesus did refer to himself as the Son of Man during his
own lifetime. This would have fitted in with his use of
the growth parables which spoke of the kingly rule of God
present in Jesus' ministry as a hidden, almost unrecog-
nisable reality, but which would later be revealed in the
full splendour of a great harvest. To correspond with this
Jesus may have spoken of himself as Son of Man in a
veiled fashion as 8:38 presents it. The attitude of people
towards Jesus and his words in the present will determine
how the future, glorious Son of Man will react to them
at the judgement. Thus there is continuity between the
present and the future, and Jesus can speak on behalf of
the Son of Man's attitude, without complete and open
identification. However, the early church made the obvious connection after the glorification of Jesus, and so the
title becomes current as a self-designation for Jesus,
whether in his lowly state of suffering or his future glorious rule.

The passage as a whole speaks of the necessity of suffering, both for Jesus himself (8:31–33) and for his followers
(34–38). This necessity is divinely willed in the case of
Jesus, and for his followers it is the only way for them to
participate in his fate. Nowhere in Jewish tradition is
there any evidence of a suffering Son of Man as the messiah. Isaiah 53, the chant of the suffering servant, does
speak of the divinely willed suffering that can make atone-
ment for the sins of the many. It is generally recognised
that his chant played an important role in enabling Jesus

to see his death in a positive way as God's act for men through him. Jesus therefore brings together two quite independent and different strands of Jewish thought, the one helping to fill out and interpret the other. The glory that belongs to the Son of Man can only be his through his willingness to give himself wholly to God's will, despite the ultimate demands that this will make on him.

A number of sayings help to explain the role of suffering for christians. Each has his *own* cross to carry. This can only be done through following Jesus, that is, imitating his self-giving and his determination to be faithful to God's call addressed to him at the baptism: 'Thou art my *well beloved* Son.' Soon we shall hear the same voice and the same designation, with the added advice for disciples 'hear ye him' (9:6). Following Jesus involves denying oneself, that is, having a change of heart, and Jesus' next saying goes on to explain the inner logic of such an apparently self-destructive policy. Saving one's life is in the end losing it. This is something we can learn at the level of everyday experience. The more we try to protect ourselves and hold on to life, the more it slips away from us. Jesus and Mark are using the idea of life in the most all-embracing way possible. It is not just a question of prolonging one's existence in this world but rather assuring an existence of another order that transcends categories of time and space. Life is the most treasured possession, the deepest reality of our existence, 'what can a man give in return for his life?' (8:37), and Jesus shows us the way to gain it, namely by losing it, that is, surrendering it to our maker, so that we might receive it back in a radically new way.

The section concludes with an eschatological ring, that is, the eternal implications of what has just been said are spelled out. Acceptance of Jesus and his words now, despite the apparent incongruity when judged by the standards of this sinful age, will mean being accepted by the glorious Son of Man when he comes (8 : 38). A concluding saying (9 : 1) would seem to indicate that this meeting of the present evil age and the future kingdom would take place within the present generation. This is one of the more difficult verses in the gospel. As a genuine saying of Jesus it indicates that he expected the final manifestation of God's kingdom within the very near future. As we shall see later the church represented by Mark had not abandoned that hope and expectation. This meant that the call of Jesus was all the more urgent now, and at the same time it was a source of great consolation for the persecuted christians. For Mark's readers it serves as an introduction to what follows, the transfiguration, which is seen as an anticipation of the end which is expected, and already realised, in the resurrection of Jesus.

1. Can you explain why Peter is called Satan merely for thinking the thoughts of men in his reaction to the idea of Jesus' suffering?

2. How does one save one's life by 'losing' it? Have you experienced the truth of this personally?

3. How do we interpret the message of apocalyptic literature for today?

Mk 9:2–8. The transfiguration

This scene is, as we have said, introduced by 9 : 1; it is an anticipated coming of the kingdom of God in power to encourage the disciples to continue on the way. The scene is clearly related to the baptism since the voice from heaven utters the same message. Now however it is no longer a message for Jesus alone, but rather an announcement for the disciples. The scene as a whole is described after the fashion of an old testament theophany, or divine appearance. The 'very high mountain' recalls Moses' meeting with Yahweh, Ex 19:3; 24:4; 32:15; the cloud is always an important element in such scenes to describe the sense of awe and mystery that surrounds the occasion, eg Ex 19:16; 40:34 f; Ezek 10:3–4; Dan 7:13; the glory of the transfigured Jesus and the exceeding brightness of his garments is indicative of the divine quality of his person (cf Ex 34:29). The whole scene is surrounded by a mysterious and awesome atmosphere that characterises it as a startling experience of the divine and it attempts to describe in human language what is really indescribable.

Clearly the event is directed to the disciples' understanding: Jesus is transfigured *before them*. The presence of Moses and Elijah is probably meant to indicate the witness of the old testament, both law and prophets, to Jesus. The disciples, as well as Jesus, are enveloped by the cloud and so taken into the divine relationship. Yet Mark, more than the other evangelists, highlights their utter lack of understanding of the experience. Fear and bewilderment are the constant reaction to any manifestation of the divine when faith is lacking (4:41; 5:42; 6:52). Here Peter shows his lack of comprehension by asking to build three tabernacles, since in all probability this betrayed a desire to 'hold on' to this moment of Jesus' glorification, something that is not permitted before the transformation of his death.

1. What could the transfiguration have meant to Jesus personally at this point in his ministry?

2. What would be the parallels in a contemporary believer's religious life to the disciples' experience and reaction?

Mk 9:9–13. Return to earth

The descent from the mountain and the subsequent discussion follow typically Markan lines, even though the topic of 9:11–13 is only loosely connected with 9:9 f, possibly due to the reference to Elijah in the transfiguration story itself. Mark, in line with the disciples' reaction on the mountain, emphasises their utter incomprehension, something that both Luke and Matthew drop completely. The command to tell no one what they had seen is in line with Mark's secrecy motif elsewhere. Publicisation of this isolated event would totally obscure the fate that lies ahead for the Son of Man as already predicted. Indeed the very idea of 'resurrection from the dead' seems obscure to them despite the fact that it was a familiar concept in late Jewish apocalyptic. When subsequently Jesus was raised the early church as a whole understood the event and interpreted it in the light of such expectation (cf Mt 27:52; 1 Cor 15:16). The fact that Peter and his associates cannot call on such a conceptual background at this point shows how ill equipped their mental processes are to understand the significance of the events in which they are participating and how timely the command to silence was.

The reference to John the Baptist's fate as the Elijah who was to come (Mal 4:5) but who has been so ill treated, serves to introduce the suffering fate of the Son of Man, of which John's death was a type (Mk 6:13–29). The fact that the Baptist's death is already a *fait accompli* merely serves to underline the near approach of Jesus' own fate and the utter rejection that lies ahead.

1. What does the resurrection of the dead mean for you?
2. Explain the command to silence as an instruction from Mark to his readers at this point of the narrative.

Mk 9:14–29. Jesus and Satan again

A mere glance at the other gospel accounts of this incident will show how drawn out the story is in Mark, because of his special interest in the drama between Jesus and Satan. Once again Mark makes a distinction between the disciples and the crowd at large, even though the latter show their enthusiasm and external attachment to Jesus, a typical feature of Mark's presentation, as we have seen. The awful plight of the boy and the pathetic reaction of the father who is significantly described as 'one of the crowd' are emphasised and illustrated by an actual description of the boy's reaction on being brought into the presence of Jesus. The subsequent dialogue between Jesus and the father merely highlights the violent and dramatic nature of the incident. Yet the whole story is related in the style and manner of a liturgical action in which the demon is addressed in solemn, cultic language (9:25). The need for faith is stressed more than once if the action is to be successful (9:23 f) and the initial reaction of Jesus on meeting with the failure of the disciples to cast out the demon is to utter a prophetic cry about 'a faithless generation'. The father of the boy must distinguish himself from the enthusiastic crowd and engage in personal dialogue with the saviour before the action can succeed, since Jesus must never be seen merely in the role of a magical wonder worker or approached in that way. Finally the boy is described by the bystanders as dead after the convulsions of the parting demon, but Mark emphasises that Jesus took him by the hand and raised him up and 'he arose'.

Coming so soon after the professed ignorance of the disciples concerning the resurrection from the dead one can only feel that Mark wanted to describe for his own readers what this idea involved—Christ's victory over the powers of evil. Yet one can see, almost at the surface of the story, the liturgical and sacramental life of the church coming into play. It is as though Mark wants to stress that this very power and victory of the risen one is now to be found in the sacramental action of the church. In all probability the exorcisms of an early baptismal rite are reflected here, since baptism was understood as the sacrament of dying and rising with Christ (cf Rom 6). This conclusion is also indicated by the amazing parallels both in structure and language between Mark's version of this story and John's account of the raising of Lazarus (Jn 11), a story which had clear baptismal overtones in the early church. The final explanation to the disciples, characteristically in the house, explains the need for prayer and fasting for the effective use of such a sacrament. In other words community participation is required, not in terms of an enthusiastic but faithless mob, but rather as genuine recognition by the whole community that God's action and man's faith (expressed in prayer and fasting) must combine for an effective operation of the church's sacraments.

1. How have the details of this story helped you to understand the meaning of the church's sacraments?

2. Determine the parallels with John 11. What does this teach you about the formation of the gospels?

Mk 9:30–32. Second prediction of the passion

The violent death that awaits Jesus in Jerusalem is predicted for a second time and again it is addressed to the disciples on their own. The secrecy motif is again operative since the message is addressed to those who have yet to engage themselves fully in the fate of the master. Only then will their discipleship be of the right kind since they will have shown their willingness to participate in that fate. However, their reaction now is typically feeble and not based on faith. Consequently they are afraid to ask Jesus to explain himself. Fear and faith that is genuine cannot coexist, and so we find repeatedly that Mark speaks of the disciples being afraid when they meet with Jesus or are confronted with some manifestation of his person or mission.

1. Explain the secrecy motif as employed by Mark in this passage.

2. Why does faith exclude fear?

Mk 9:33–50. Further instruction on the nature of discipleship

Each of the three predictions of the passion are followed by reactions of the disciples that show how they have failed utterly to comprehend what they have just heard. This inevitably leads on to a further explanation of suffering as a general principle of discipleship: 'if anyone would . . .' (8:34; 9:34; 10:43). What Jesus is declaring as his own fate has a universal significance for all would-be disciples.

The composition of this section is a good example of the way in which the words of Jesus were remembered and transmitted in the oral period that preceded the gospel writing. Sayings which originally were not related in meaning are strung together like beads by a series of interlocking hook words; 'in my name' (9:37, 39, 41) 'to give scandal' (9:42–48); 'fire' (9:48, 49) salt—salted (9:49, 50). This is a normal enough technique for remembering sayings even though they may not have a strict thematic unity. However Mark clearly does see the whole section as bearing on the question at issue, the division among the disciples, since he rounds it off on the note of 'being at peace with one another'.

1. The starting point for the discussion is the lack of harmony among the disciples which shows itself in squabbling over positions of honour within the group. Once again the discussion in Mark takes place 'in the house', one of the favourite places for the special instruction of the little group, and Jesus adopts the position of the rabbi seated with the circle of disciples around him (here identified with the twelve). Such dissension is a clear indication that they are still thinking on a very human level about Christ and his role, something that will emerge more clearly in the request of the sons of Zebedee after the third prediction of the passion (10:35–37). Their failure relates to a false understanding of Jesus as a political messiah of this world and Jesus seeks to correct their misconceptions by pointing to the true nature of his life and mission. When questioned about their discussions they remain silent, obviously aware of their failure once they are questioned by Jesus. When he is present it is obvious, even to them, how ridiculous their human aspirations are and how ill they fit in with all that has gone before. Jesus uses the example of a little child, the symbol of helplessness, to correct the attitude and to illustrate the basic principle of his life and that of his disciple: one must be prepared to forget oneself completely and abandon any idea of self-glorification. The idea of service is taken further with 9:37 through the identification of Christ with the little child, and ultimately with God himself— service of a little child becomes service of Christ and God —an idea that is further developed in the judgement scene of Matthew (Mt 25:31–45).

1. What does it mean today to 'receive a child in the name of Christ'? Give some concrete examples.

2. How can the principle of discipleship, the requirement to 'be least of all and servant of all', be practised in today's world?

2. Verses 38–42 take up the idea of acting in the name of Jesus. Interestingly enough Jesus does not confine even the casting out of demons to those officially designated to carry on this aspect of his ministry. 'He that is not against us is for us' is his way of judging such activity. There is a shared responsibility for keeping Christ's name, that is his person and his power, alive and active, and whoever engages in the struggle against the forces of evil, which Christ has successfully waged, cannot be regarded as an enemy of the gospel. Already such a one has accepted the gospel message. Here is ecumenism in practice, and the recognition that similar good works, even when they appear to come from different sources, have both a common origin and goal which we should recognise.

What lesson does this passage give us about judging ecumenical activity today?

3. Serving others is the ultimate criterion of discipleship but being a stumbling block to others is the very negation of all that Christ stands for. In these verses we meet the strong sense of reaction which is characteristic of Jesus' words. The two ultimate alternatives open to man are here placed clearly before the disciples: 'entering into life' or 'entering the kingdom of God' stand over against being cast into hell. In face of these alternatives there is only one reasonable course for anyone to adopt, that is to abandon whatever proves an obstacle either to self or to

another in opting for the kingdom or for life. The principle already enunciated about 'losing one's life to save it'
(8:34) is illustrated here in the most striking fashion with
reference to the organs of the body, even the most vital
ones. The description that is here given of hell has to be
understood in relation to the word used, *Gehenna,* which
is a Greek form of the Hebrew for the Valley of Hinnom,
a horrific place outside Jerusalem. This place had been
notorious for child sacrifice during the reigns of the two
apostate kings, Ahaz and Manasseh, in the sixth century
BC. Subsequently it became the city dump, a place of
decay and smouldering, the very opposite of life, and was
often mentioned in late Jewish sources as a place of punishment in the after-life. Fire as a form of punishment
was also quite frequently mentioned, and the phrase of
9:48 'where their worm does not die and the fire is not
quenched' is taken from Is 66:24 as a description for the
unceasing torments of Israel's enemies when Yahweh will
vindicate his own. Thus Jesus uses contemporary images
and expressions to describe the hell that is in store for the
man who excludes himself from God. While traditional
teaching and preaching has often overstressed these details as though they were descriptive accounts of the state
or place of punishment, nothing should take away from
the emphatic and direct force of Jesus' position—a man
can cut himself off from life and from the kingdom
through his abuse of his fellow man.

*1. How does one explain the doctrine of hell meaning-
fully for today's world?*

*2. How might one translate the realism of Jesus' langu-
age in regard to scandal without understanding it with
strict literalism?*

4. The final three sayings are all linked together by the word 'salt' and it is rather difficult to see exactly how they fit in with the previous themes. However salt can have a twofold effect. On the one hand its cutting and stinging quality makes it a suitable image for punishment, 'everyone will be salted with fire' (9:49), and this relates to the previous theme. On the other hand salt is also a preservative whose taste and protective quality make it a suitable metaphor for life in its purity and goodness, and so these sayings also take up the first theme about genuine discipleship. At the beginning of the sermon on the mount Matthew has a saying similar to that of Mark, addressed to disciples and describing them as the salt of the earth, which at the same time indicates the danger of their losing their saltness (Mt 5:13). Here in Mark the emphasis is on the latter aspect, the danger of the group of disciples losing their savour by allowing pettiness and quarrels to disrupt the real unity that should come from their mutual service of one another. That is the only way to true and lasting peace.

1. Describe those qualities in a contemporary christian community that would correspond with the dangers to genuine discipleship described in these verses.

2. How could a modern community be said to have salt in it?

Mk 10:1–31. Further instruction for disciples
The scene changes now as we leave Galilee and move to Transjordan on the way up to Jerusalem. Jesus has already explained the radical nature of discipleship and once there is still willingness on the part of the disciples to go to Jerusalem there is need for further instruction

on various questions that will arise within any community of disciples—divorce, children, riches and reward for discipleship. In treating of such specific questions the basic issue of discipleship will emerge again in all its clarity and demanding quality.

1. *10 : 2–11. On divorce.* Mark's presentation of the divorce question is simple and straightforward by comparison with Matthew, who introduces a contemporary debate between different rabbinical circles on what was a legitimate ground for divorce according to Deut 24:1–4 (Mt 19:1–9). In both cases the reply of Jesus is clear and unequivocal—marriage is one by the design of the creator and accordingly divorce as permitted in the law of Moses is a temporary prescription related to a particular situation that is not part of God's original creation. Now with the coming of Jesus things must be restored to their original condition, since the kingdom which he preaches is the restoration of the original will and plan of God for man. When the radical nature of Christ's claim on his disciple is applied to this fundamental area of human life, marriage, the result is a total and lifelong commitment of the partners to each other, as the only suitable expression of the creator's will for the universe expressed in the beginning and now repeated through the restoration of all things in Christ.

1. Explain how the nature of marriage as monogamous is made clear in the light of Christ's ministry.

2. Should the church today recognise the hardness of our hearts by not legislating against divorce but rather by presenting the christian ideal of marriage?

2. *10 : 12–16. Christ and children.* The question of the little children being presented to Jesus is a suitable

opportunity for again touching on the question of the attitude of the genuine disciple already treated earlier at 9:36 f. They must be open and willing to serve the needs of the little ones, who typify the helpless ones of this world, realising how close they are to Jesus. And further they should themselves have the trusting, humble, unselfconscious attitude of little children in regard to the gift of the kingdom which is being offered to them.

As well as serving to illustrate the nature of discipleship many commentators see in this passage a reflection of the baptismal liturgy of the early church. A phrase such as 'suffer the little children to come to me and do not prevent them', has echoes of similar formulae which admitted candidates to baptism (Acts 8:36). Besides the action of Jesus at the end is portrayed in a cultic fashion, as though Jesus were seen to authenticate the practice of the early church in regard to infant baptism. The question of infant baptism is today a very current one with the churches, as witnessed by the theological controversy on the matter in the German Evangelical church, and the new rite of infant baptism for Roman catholics. While the arguments against a mechanistic and quasi-magical use of the sacrament are very valid the tradition of infant baptism is a very old one in the church and may well have its roots as far back as this piece of early material which Mark has used here.

1. How do you explain the practice of infant baptism in the church?

2. How does the attitude of Jesus towards children as portrayed here throw light on the matter?

3. *10:17–26. Christ and riches.* This is perhaps the most impressive piece of narrative in the whole of Mark's gospel. The author tells the story with great feeling for the

situation and brings all his powers of description to play on the various human emotions that are involved in the confrontation between Jesus and the rich man with the dumb-founded disciples serving as an audience to the discussion. Clearly for Mark the story touches on the kernel of the problem of discipleship as experienced by his readers—the problem of riches. Significantly, the discussion takes place, Mark reminds us, as Jesus was 'setting out on *his* journey'. The instruction for disciples can never be divorced from Jesus or his life, something that was not lost on Paul who writes: 'For you know the grace of our Lord Jesus Christ, that though he was rich, yet *for your sake* he became poor, so that by his poverty you might become rich' (2 Cor 8:9).

The man approaches Jesus with great enthusiasm and respect, kneeling before him and addressing him as 'Good Master'. Jesus immediately rejects the description, because he wishes to direct the man's attention away from any over-enthusiastic acceptance of himself without due consideration of whom he represents, namely, God and his kingdom. It has been noted that in enumerating the various commandments Jesus mentions all the negative ones with the addition of honouring one's father and mother. The man has no problem in declaring that he has observed all these from his youth since really he has been quite meticulous in avoiding any evil. Now, however, the real challenge of being a follower of Jesus is presented to him. Jesus loves him and so issues the radical invitation: is he prepared to leave all his riches behind and follow him? Mark gives us his response with a really poignant touch—his face fell and he left sorrowfully. Here was a man generous in avoiding evil but not prepared to answer the call of love, the call to go and do something positive. Here was the personal tragedy of the grace of Jesus' call rejected.

Realising that it was attachment to his possessions that really closed this man's heart to the call, Jesus twice declares how hard it is for those who have riches to enter the kingdom of God: indeed it is humanly impossible, since the lure of wealth can make a man totally blind to the true realities. Twice Mark reiterates the astonishment of the disciples, so accustomed are they from their Jewish background to identify wealth and possessions with God's favour and blessings. Here they have come face to face with the radically new standard of Jesus' gospel—a standard that rejects the accepted, external criteria of judaism. Indeed so radical and so demanding is this standard that it is dependent on God's action and not man's achievement for its observance. The demand of God's kingdom is measured only by the gift of God's power that it brings with it, if only people would accept the word of Jesus.

1. Explain fully the difference of attitude between the religious mentality of the rich man and the demand of Jesus.

2. Why is it impossible for a rich man to enter the kingdom of heaven? How does God's grace make it possible?

4. *10:28–31. Rewards of discipleship.* Peter, as spokesman for the disciples who have not refused the call, now puts the obvious question: what reward will they have? Jesus' answer is clear and unequivocal, yet not without its own challenge to their preconceived ideas. In answering the call of Jesus they have been separated not merely from earthly possessions, but even from family ties. Mark's readers could verify for themselves within their own community how true Jesus' promise was that they would be

rewarded a hundredfold even in this life for such loyalty.
They have accepted the gospel which is about Jesus (1:1)
and so these words are addressed to them also. The sharing of goods held in common, and the deep sense of
brotherhood experienced, were real rewards for accepting the call of Jesus and listening to the gospel about him.
But it is not just a question of rewards in the popular
sense, for persecution too is promised, as these Roman
readers are very well aware. Neither must they seek their
fulfilment in merely this-world terms since a greater
future, the life of the age to come, is promised. This was
the very question that had bothered the rich man (10:17),
the question that bothers every man and predisposes him
to seek for an answer from Jesus. Those who have followed him now have their deepest quest answered, but
with the warning that they must never presume on God's
gift or reckon with their own achievement as meriting
what they will be given. 'Many that are first will be last'
is a timely warning for the presumptuous Peter.

*1. What have you learned from the reply to Peter about
your attempts to merit everlasting life?*

*2. Do christians receive a hundredfold in this life? If
not, why not?*

Mk 10:32–34. Third prediction of the passion

Mark rounds off the first scene with the third announcement of the passion, to be followed by the usual unveiling
of the misconceptions of those who follow. Once again we
are reminded that Jesus is on the way, and the picture
painted as a setting for this announcement is full of meaning. Jesus goes ahead, he is the leader and like every
leader he is alone. Future events are now casting their

shadow and the disciples are bewildered (literally 'they were in agony') and afraid, yet somehow the magnetism of Jesus draws them on. The circumstances of what lies ahead are clearly unfolded now, and the mockery and scourging are new details that fill out the grim picture. Yet the disciples can be described as following, however little they are ready for the final catastrophe.

Explain the human relationships and attitudes that Mark envisages by his description of the setting in this passage.

Mk 10:35–40. The request of the sons of Zebedee

Once more a concrete incident is used by Mark to illustrate the blindness of the disciples to the role Jesus now clearly sees for himself. James and John seek a special place in the kingdom. From the way their request is presented it is not clear how they understand the kingdom. What is clear is that their request is personally motivated, even to the way in which they try to twist Jesus' arm by the very form of their question. However they understand the nature of the kingdom, presumably as a political one, they are not prepared for the suffering that must go with it. And even if they are prepared to share his chalice (his passion) and his baptism (his death) they must realise that to share in the glory of Jesus' exaltation is still a gift from the Father, something that Jesus himself would not claim as his own. Timely words indeed for the would-be martyr for the kingdom both then and now!

1. In what way do you feel yourself reproached by the attitude and prayer of the two disciples?
2. What is the lesson of Jesus' reply for us today?

Mk 10:41–45. Final instruction on the nature of discipleship

As on the two previous occasions Jesus has to explain the matter further since there is still a very human approach to him and his mission in evidence among the disciples. The ten are indignant, not because the two brothers have failed to grasp what Jesus had been saying, but rather because they have anticipated their own wishes in seeking places of honour and authority in the coming kingdom. Accordingly this particular instruction is addressed to those who seek authority or are given special positions within the community of disciples. The twelve are already aware that they have been granted such a position, but this does not dispense them from the call to discipleship; indeed it makes the supreme demand on them, as Jesus' own life and ministry bear witness.

The standard of the world for those in authority is to lord it over their subjects, a standard clearly shared by the twelve. However, Jesus points to a very different standard which he himself exemplifies perfectly. The one in authority must be prepared to be the slave and servant of all. This service does not just consist in performing menial tasks on behalf of the group. Rather it must be based on the attitude of Jesus himself, who seeks no honour or recognition but looks instead for ways of giving himself for others, culminating in the actual giving of his life for them. The expression of 10:45 is based on a very famous passage in the old testament, the chant of the suffering servant (Is 53) who willingly gives his life on behalf of the many. Jesus considers his life and his impending death from this point of view. This is the greatest service he can give his fellow-man, and at the same time it is the greatest claim he can make on them. His authority

is his authenticity, that is his utter selflessness on behalf
of others, in accordance with the gospel he preaches.

*1. How should authority be exercised so that it can be
seen to be real service in a community?*
2. How does the example of Jesus illustrate this role?
*3. What are the temptations for the church to adopt
the standards of the world in the exercise of authority?*

Mk 10:41–45. Final illustration on the nature of discipleship

The crowd begins to gather as Jesus and his band of followers approach their destination. Mark, it would seem,
wishes to conclude this section with a miracle about seeing, just as earlier the healing of the blind man served as
a prelude to Peter's confession. A number of indications
in the account shows that Mark wishes to portray in this
story certain features of discipleship which are still missing in his followers. Bar Timaeus, the blind man, responds instantly on *hearing* that Jesus was passing, by
making his request. His promptness is equally evident
when Jesus calls him. Significantly the title he uses for
Jesus is quite inadequate as a full description of him or
his mission, for it was by far the most popular designation
of the messiah among the ordinary people. Yet this lack of
theoretic knowledge about Jesus in no way hinders him
from making his urgent request. Mark does not insist on
the secrecy theme at this point since the example of the
blind man and his request for sight is a pointer to all who
hope to understand the events about to take place. Instead of being sent home Bar Timaeus follows Jesus in the
way, the way that leads to full disclosure of his person.
An open receptive spirit that seeks no favour from Jesus

except 'to see' is the ideal disposition for the disciple at
this point. Bar Timaeus is an example to all.

*1. From a theological point of view how do you explain
the absence of secrecy in regard to this miracle?*
*2. What is there about the faith of Bar Timaeus that
makes him an acceptable example for would-be disciples?*

6

Scene two: judgement on Jerusalem
Mk 11:1–13:37

Jesus has now arrived at Jerusalem, the city of revelation. Already the city is associated with hostility to him (3:1) and now that he arrives there we find him aware of this opposition and so passing judgement on it 11:1–12:12. The five controversies that follow only heighten the tension between Jesus and the Jewish religious leaders, and to round off this scene Jesus announces the destruction of Jerusalem and the future glory of the Son of Man as a message of hope to terrified disciples threatened with persecution. Throughout almost the whole of this scene Jesus alone is at the centre of the stage. The disciples on whom the previous section was totally concentrated now form a passive audience observing what happened to Jesus in his confrontation with his enemies.

Mk 11:1–11. The messianic entry
All the gospels relate an enthusiastic entry of Jesus into Jerusalem at this point. This is seen as a fulfilment of various old testament prophecies which speak of the messianic king coming to Mount Sion, eg Zech 9:9 and 14:4. David's son returns to his father's city. The evangelists see a certain amount of tragic irony in the situation that an enthusiastic welcome turns out to be a total rejection in the space of a few days. Yet the ways of God are seen in

all this, because the enthronment of Jesus takes place in a totally unexpected way, by his exaltation to God's right hand, an insight which St John exploits to the full in his passion narrative. Jesus' entry is a prophetic action intended to shock Jerusalem into the realisation of who he is. The people are on the whole enthusiastic and rejoice at the coming kingdom of David without explicitly identifying this with Jesus. However, Mark does not overelaborate on the scene.

How do you explain the sudden disappearance of the crowd in Mark's presentation?

Mk 11:12–14 and 20–25. The cursing of the barren fig-tree

This is perhaps one of the most uncharacteristic actions of Jesus that we find recorded in the gospels, that is, if we are to take it literally. Jesus normally refuses to use his power in this kind of magical way. Indeed there are signs that it was a certain embarrassment for Mark himself (certainly it was for Luke, who omits it altogether) for he uses it as an example for the efficacy of prayer addressed to God with faith (11:20–25). The act of cursing the fig-tree may be seen as a symbolic act of judgement against unfaithful Israel, so often described by the image of a fig tree in the old testament (Jer 8:13; Joel 1:7; Ezek 17:24). Besides, Jesus himself spoke a parable about the fig-tree that bore no fruit (Lk 13:6–9) but which was given another chance due to the entreaties of the gardener. Here the condemnation is for foliage without fruit, which when applied to Israel means appearances without any substance. Now the time for clemency is over and judgement must be passed.

The little discourse on prayer which Mark introduces

at this point stresses the need for faith, and concludes with the idea of forgiveness of the brother as a prelude to speaking to the Father. There is an echo here of one of the petitions of the 'Our Father' and so this strange scene of judgement is shown by Mark to be divinely willed and not the result of petulance or rancour on the part of Jesus.

Explain the intimate connection there is between judgement and salvation.

Mk 11:15–19; 27–33. Cleansing the temple and the authority of Jesus

Once again the action of Jesus must be seen as a judgement on the temple, or at least on those who worship there and their attitudes. The expected messiah was thought of as somebody who would restore Israelite worship to its original purity, so that the action of Jesus is both judging and saving. Mark emphasises that the temple is to be a house of prayer *for all the nations*. The distinction between the court of the gentiles and that of the Jews has to be broken down, something that is realised in the body of Christ, the new spiritual temple, where there is no distinction between Jew and Greek, slave and free.

Jesus is subsequently questioned about the authority for his actions but refuses to give a direct answer. Instead he questions his accusers with a view to getting them to recognise the source of his authority. They should have recognised that the baptism of John was 'from above' and likewise that Jesus' authority had its source with God. But he refuses to be pressed further on the point. That will eventually be made manifest to all.

What was the role of the temple in Israel's worship and how is the body of Christ the new temple?

Mk 12:1–12. The parable of the wicked husbandmen

It has sometimes been suggested that this parable was not spoken by Jesus himelf but was composed later by the early church to try to explain his rejection and to integrate it with the overall pattern of Israel's rejection of all God's ambassadors in history. However, the genuine parables of Jesus all have their source and inspiration in the homely, everyday life of the country. This parable too fits such a context and so there is no reason for not attributing it to Jesus. Much of the land of Palestine was owned by absentee landlords, and agrarian unrest was tantamount to an expression of nationalism. The point of the story originally was to challenge the Jews in regard to the rejection of the landowner's son, for the land of Israel was Yahweh's gift to his people, and in the prophets Israel is often described as the Lord's vineyard (Is 5:1–7). Mark has preserved and pointed this meaning by describing the son as 'the well beloved' one, which was the designation of him by the voice from heaven at the baptism and transfiguration (1:10; 9:6). Furthermore he has applied to the whole story a section of Ps 118:22 ff, 'the stone rejected by the builders has become the corner-stone' which was a text that was often used by the apostolic church to explain the exaltation of Jesus by God after the apparent failure of the death (Acts 4:1; 1 Pet 2:7; Eph 2:20). Coming at this point in Mark's narrative it is an accusation against the Jewish leaders that in rejecting Jesus they are rejecting God's special ambassador, a point that is not lost on them as Mark carefully notes. At the same time the reader is given a further insight into Jesus' vocation as the 'well-beloved son'. It is a title that does not shield him from danger, but rather exposes him more fully to the hatred of God's enemies.

How do you explain the action of the Father in exposing his son to danger? (See Rom 5 : 1–10)

Mk 12:13–44. Controversies

A series of controversies follow, that point to the authority of Jesus on the one hand, and the hostility of his opponents on the other. Yet all is not bleak for there is the kindly scribe who is impressed by Jesus' answering of his opponents and the poor widow whose generosity is highlighted by her poverty. Both serve as useful instruction for the disciples.

1. *12 : 13–17. Tribute to Caesar.* To understand the dilemma that Jesus' enemies wished to pose him we must appreciate that the coin with Caesar's image and inscription was a tax-coin that reminded loyal Jews of their subjection to the hated Roman imperial rule. Therefore a direct answer by Jesus would involve him in either national disloyalty or political subversion. The dilemma remained actual for christians up to the edict of Constantine, and of course was of particular importance to Mark's readers, christians in Nero's Rome, whose refusal to take part in emperor worship was seen as an act of political insubordination. Jesus' reply is not an evasion of the question but a challenge to his enquirers to consider the relative importance of the question they have posed as compared with the ultimate question of a man's relations with God. In any case by calling for a coin of tribute he already indicates to them their practical acceptance of Caesar. The force of Jesus' reply is not to set up two independent realms, Caesar's and God's, but to

point out the secondary nature of their question by comparison with the allegiance to God which he called for. The first part of the reply would have answered their question but instead Jesus puts the emphasis on the second, 'render to God the things that are God's'. Thus what was really a political question is put into a religious context and thereby made relative.

The question about payment of lawful taxes is not in itself unimportant, as Jesus showed on another occasion (Mt 17:24–27), but by comparison with the demands of God's kingdom that has drawn near to men made in the image of God it is of secondary significance.

1. What should the christian's attitude be towards payment of taxes?

2. What do you think of Jesus' technique in answering the cunning question of his opponents?

2. 12:18–27. The resurrection. Behind this question lies a theological controversy between the two great religious sects of judaism at the time, the Sadducees and the Pharisees. The former were a wealthy, powerful class who had accepted the standards and attitudes of Greek civilization as it had touched religious and social life in Palestine. The Pharisees on the other hand were the heirs to the *hasîdîm* or pious ones of the Maccabean wars, who had resisted any such external influences. It was in these circles that the idea of the resurrection emerged for the first time. The just ones who had died in loyalty to Yahweh would eventually share in the messianic blessings to come. Here the Sadducees put their position forcibly by attempting to show how ridiculous the very idea of resurrection is.

Jesus' reply is twofold, and points out where the real

source of their difficulty lies. They have a far too human, this-world understanding of what the resurrection involves, and more important still they do not realise the power of God. Resurrection is not resuscitation to life as it is known and experienced here, and therefore not to be judged by the criteria we would normally apply to such a possibility. Secondly, the scriptures show *that* the resurrection is a real possibility, for God reveals himself to Moses as the God of Abraham, Isaac and Jacob, the three great patriarchs of Israel. The fact that Yahweh speaks of himself in this way shows clearly that the patriarchs still live with him and that the relationship between them and the living God is an everlasting one as far as God is concerned. Such a God can only be described as the God of the living, and so the Sadducees have really erred in not recognising the power of God, a power that extends to life and death.

Do you understand the idea of the resurrection as a new creation, or are you guilty of some of the errors of the Sadducees?

3. *12 : 28–34. The love command.* The discussion concerning the love command has a different emphasis in Mark from either Luke or Matthew. The question was often debated among the rabbis whether the various prescriptions of the law, 613 in all at the time of Christ, could be classified or reduced to a few basic ones. As such it need not be a controversial question, but both Matthew and Luke see the posing of this question as a test of Jesus. In Mark, however, it is an honest enquirer, impressed by the answer of Jesus to the Sadducees, who asks his opinion on the matter. Besides, Mark has quite a long section at the end in which the questioner approves of Jesus' reply,

quoting scripture (1 Sam 15:22) to show that care for one's brother is more acceptable to God than any sacrifice. The whole section in Mark is therefore an instruction for disciples rather than a controversy with opponents.

Jesus' reply to the question posed shows his authority as interpreter of God's will by comparison with the ordinary scribes who felt obliged to treat every jot and tittle of the law as equally binding and important. In his answer Jesus shows himself to be at heart anti-legalistic. Love is the supreme law of the christian life with its twofold expression in terms of love of God and love of the neighbour. Both expressions are found already in the old testament, Deut 6:5 and Lev 19:18, yet nowhere in judaism do we find them brought together so emphatically or highlighted so clearly as summing up God's will for his people. Accordingly, Jesus has removed these prescriptions of the Pentateuch from the category of *law* as such, and instead has made love the determining *attitude* of his disciples in the community of the kingdom. Because the scribe has assented to this he too is invited to join the community.

1. Explain why love should be the only 'law' of the kingdom as preached by Jesus. Why is it more important than all sacrifice?

2. How are the two commands inter-related? How do they relate to the single 'new commandment' of Jn 13:34?

4. *12:35–37. Concerning David's son.* The arguments in this section may not appear totally convincing to our minds, but to a Jew brought up on the absolute binding force of scripture it has a particular force. The question at issue concerns the status of 'the Christ', which

means literally 'the anointed one'. Originally, as we have seen, 'Christ' was not a proper name but a Greek designation of the office known in Hebrew as the messiah. By far the most popular understanding of the messiah's role was that he would be the son of David, on the basis of 2 Sam 7, where Yahweh promised to David an everlasting dynasty. Unfortunately this promise became associated with a political liberator of Israel, a role Jesus refused to accept or fulfil, as we have also seen. By posing the question Jesus is not directly speaking about himself but wishes to correct the distortion of the idea of the messiah that was current. He does so by citing from Ps 110, a psalm that was understood to refer to the messiah and which was believed to have been written by David. If David calls the messiah 'Lord' and not just 'Son', as he does in this psalm, the only conclusion is that he is more than David's son.

Mark uses this story to clarify further the role of Jesus, who already has been recognised and professed as the Christ by Peter on behalf of the disciples (8:29). However, subsequent events have shown how unwilling they are to recognise anything but the accepted role of political liberator for Jesus.

1. By following the story of Jesus to this point how has your personal understanding of him and his mission been deepened or changed?

2. Why was Jesus unwilling to accept the role of political liberator?

5. *12:37b–44. The scribes and the widow.* This section brings to a conclusion Jesus' confrontation with the teachers of Israel, the scribes. At this point Matthew introduces a sweeping denunciation of the scribes and

Pharisees and their hypocritical attitudes (Mt 23), but Mark with a few short swift strokes paints an equally effective picture. They seek prominence and recognition at every possible opportunity, using their position as official interpreters of the law to impose on simple people. In particular they show their true attitude by the way in which they fawn on helpless widows, who were supposed to be protected by Jewish law. And all this despite a sanctimonious attitude of devotion to prayer and ritual.

The mention of widows is the cue for the very touching contrast that Mark gives us to this debauched sense of religious duty. A poor widow is seen approaching one of the collection boxes in the outer courtyard and gives her contribution to the upkeep of the temple and its service. The amount she gave was worth just a few pence in our money, yet because it was all she had it was of infinite price. She was giving her life's means and that meant everything to her.

1. Why is there a constant danger for ministers of religion to become like the scribes?

2. Explain why the woman's generosity is so lauded at this point in the gospel.

Mk 13:1–34. The victory of the Son of Man

The drama is rapidly approaching its climax and all that now remains is that the Son of Man should go through with the divine purpose he has already recognised and accepted. However, before the fateful hour it is important that this suffering Son of Man should be shown in his true colours, as the glorious, other-world figure who will gather his elect from the four corners of the earth in a triumphant celebration. Chapter 13, the so-called apocalyptic discourse, is an anticipated presentation of this victory of the Son of Man, something Jesus himself will allude to at the moment of trial (14:62). It is an important reminder for Mark's readers not to lose heart, since they will shortly be asked to make their profession of faith in Jesus, the Son of God, as he lies dead on the cross (15:39). It is also a message of hope for them in their own situation that despite the persecution and suffering of the present, they will eventually share in the victory of the Son of Man if they are not deceived by false Christs and do not become slothful in their waiting for his return.

This chapter has often been described as 'the little apocalypse' since it betrays many of the features of apocalyptic. Certainly much of the imagery, the signs and the description of the final destruction are definitely apocalyptic in their tone and colouring. However, there are other features too; the warnings of 13:9-13 are found in the missionary discourse in Matthew (Mt 10:9-16) and in isolation are not necessarily related to the end of the age. It is better, therefore, to describe the chapter as a farewell victory speech of Jesus (great characters such as Jacob and Moses gave similar orations before death) with apocalyptic colouring and tone.

In Jewish expectation the coming of the messiah or messianic times (however different circles understood it) would mark the end of the present evil age. In apocalyptic circles, where such ideas as the kingdom of God and the resurrection of the dead were in vogue, ideas which Jesus shared and interpreted in the light of his own ministry, the age to come involved the destruction of the present world and the making of a new heaven and earth. We have already seen how Jesus' parables of the kingdom dealt with the same problem, and explained the claim that with him the kingdom of God had come, despite the absence of the apocalyptic manifestations that were to be expected. The early church for a time accepted this tension once it had seen the claim of Jesus, that with him the new age had dawned, authenticated through his resurrection (Acts 3:21). It is clear from many of the new testament writings, eg the epistles of Paul to the Thessalonians, that the delay in Christ's return soon became a real problem for them. In the meantime christians are not to be despondent or lax, but on their guard lest the urgency of Jesus' call for repentance and the promptness of their own response be dissipated because of the delay.

The temple and Jerusalem itself as the holy city was naturally a focal point for much Jewish speculation about the appearance of the messiah and the coming age. It was there that Yahweh 'had made his name to dwell', and it was unthinkable that it should not play a vital part in the dawning of the new age, when God would again visit his people. Older commentators believed that in this chapter Jesus is giving two distinct prophecies—the destruction of Jerusalem and the end of the world. However it is better not to make such a distinction, since from Mark's point of view at least (cf Mt 24:3) these two events coincide. If the temple at Jerusalem is to share in the new age it too must be remade, something Mark sees dramatically realised in the death of Christ, whose risen body is the new temple 'not made with hands' (Mk 14:58). In all this there is a shading of time perspective that seems strange to us who are accustomed to separate the death and resurrection of Jesus, the destruction of the temple in the year 70 AD and the end of the world yet to come. For Mark and his readers, however, all three blend into the one reality of the new age which God has inaugurated with the resurrection of his Son, and which will soon be brought to completion through his glorious return.

In composing this discourse out of various sayings of

Jesus and other pieces of tradition Mark has left a very clear imprint which enables us to understand his purpose more clearly. This imprint can be detected by taking account of the various repetitions and corresponding patterns that emerge from a close examination of the text. We suggest the following as one possible framework.

Introduction to audience (disciples) and place (Mount of Olives). A question of the disciples suggests a twofold structure: *when* shall these things take place and what shall be their *sign* (13:1–4)?

The discourse now sets out to answer these questions by giving the *signs* first (13:5–23) and telling *when* it will take place (13:28–37). These two main sections are separated by a short central section (13:24–27) which is merely an announcement about the coming Son of Man. In the opening and closing sections exhortation to believers is intermingled with the actual information given after a regular pattern outlined below:

I. The signs (announcement and exhortation)
  a Take heed . . . of false Christs (5–6)
  b When you hear . . . of wars (7–8)
  c Take heed . . . of persecutions (9–13)
  b' When you see flee . . . wars (14–20)
  a' Take heed . . . of false prophets (21–23)
II. Announcement of the coming Son of Man (24–27)
III. When? (announcement and exhortation)
  a Parable of the fig tree (28–29)
  b Saying: 'within this generation' (30)
  c Saying: solemn confirmation (31)
  b' Saying: 'we do not know the day or the hour' (32)
  a' Parable: doorkeeper watches (33–36)
Conclusion: watch (37).

According to this plan it will be noted that sections I and III correspond exactly. Each has five subdivisions built around a central statement *c* with *a* and *b* corresponding to *a′* and *b′*. Section II is the central action of the discourse, its very brevity helping to underline the important message: the Son of Man will come in glory and gather his elect.

I. *13 : 5–23. Signs and warnings for the coming age.* In all there are five signs and warnings given in this section and as already indicated *a* and *b* correspond with *a′* and *b′*. In the central and prominent position is the section on persecution.

a and a′. 13 : 5–6; 21–23. False Christs. The opening verses, 5–6, refer rather vaguely to the false Christs and the danger of the faithful being deceived. However, the corresponding verses, 21–23, make the whole matter clear. The false Christs are those who claim that they are the messiah, and who by their wondrous signs are likely to seduce a people who are easily impressed by signs of power. We have seen all through how Mark has used the secrecy motif to point to the fact that faith in Jesus as messiah is not faith in a wonder-worker but in the well beloved Son who gives his life for others. Power has always a certain fascination for people, both those who use it and those who witness it. The fact that those who rely on such displays can be described as false Christs shows how opposed such an attitude is to the true gospel of Jesus Christ, and how destructive it is of the spirit of true faith.

1. Explain what is lacking in the faith of those who are impressed by signs of power.

2. Why is the threat of false Christs a permanent one for the church and the world? How is it destroyed?

b and b'. 13:7–8 and 14–20. Wars and rumours of wars.
Throughout christian history the temptation has been to
see the events of verses 7–8 realised in one cataclysm or
another. Mark says that these are but the beginnings of
the birth pangs. It is through such events that the new
age is accomplished. The corresponding verses (14–20)
describe these events in greater detail in relation to the
fall of Jerusalem. The description by Josephus, the
Jewish historian, of the destruction wreaked by the
Roman soldiers and the terror of the fleeing Jews, shows
how these verses, many of them echoing passages from old
testament prophets threatening judgement on the unfaithful Jerusalem, were almost literally fulfilled in the
year 70 AD. The fact that the end did not come was a
shock for the faithful christians then, as we can see from
the way in which a later evangelist like Luke separates the
fall of Jerusalem from the end of the world (Lk 17:20–
37; 21:20). As far as Mark's account is concerned it
should be a warning to us against any over-literal interpretation of these verses. With Christ's victory the end is
already assured, and the presence of wars, hunger and
suffering in our world is a sign of our unredeemed humanity that has still not accepted his way or is not prepared to take his example. The important message for
christians is that God's protecting hand is there, provided
they are faithful to their calling as the elect.

*Do you consider that christians share the responsibility
for the wars and hunger of our world?*

c. 13:9–13. Persecutions. Mark obviously intends this
section as central, and it is here that he addresses himself
directly to the immediate situation of his readers. The
persecutions and trials that a christian can expect are

clearly mirrored, even the very divisions among families. All this opposition and persecution is seen as necessarily connected with the preaching of the gospel, which must first take place to all the nations. The message however is one of courage; he who perseveres to the end shall be saved. Christians must be prepared for this period until the gospel reaches all the nations, but in Mark's perspective that cannot be long, for already it has been preached in Rome, the capital of the earth. Hence the early missionary activity of the church had a note of great urgency about it—the sooner the gospel is preached the sooner Christ will return.

How could motivation for missionary activity draw its inspiration from the early church and its expectation?

II. *13:24–27. The coming of the Son of Man.* As already indicated this section is the key point of the whole discourse: the Son of Man will come in glory to gather his elect. This is the real message of hope for christians, no matter what their present situation. The passage is intimately related to Mk 8:38 where acceptance of Jesus and his words in this evil generation is seen as a guarantee of acceptance by the Son of Man in the future. Here we are given a full description of the coming Son of Man, a coming that is attended by signs in nature itself, since as Paul puts it 'the whole creation is groaning in travail' because it too will share in the glorious liberation of the sons of God (Rom 8:21 f). Many of the signs that are mentioned here are part and parcel of Jewish apocalyptic descriptions, but however strange they might appear to us in detail we should not lose sight of a basic and constant theme in the bible, namely that the universe itself shares in the ultimate destiny of man.

*1. How can the expectation of the Son of Man be made
meaningful for man today?*

*2. Have scientific discoveries made it impossible to ac-
cept the role of the universe in the drama of salvation?*

III. *13 : 28–36. When shall these things be?* Mark combines an answer to the question 'When?' posed by the disciples at the outset with further exhortation to them.
Preoccupation about the time may destroy the basic attitude which is to be watchful for the coming.

*a and a' 13 : 28 f; 33–36. Parables of fig tree and door-
keeper.* Both these parables stress the basic attitude that
should dominate the christian life, namely watchfulness.
Nature gives ample signs of its maturing to harvest time,
and so it is also with God's kingdom. On the other hand
if a person has been entrusted with a post of responsibility
by his departing master the only prudent thing is to at-
tend properly to his duties while he is away. Both belong
to the category of parables of the kingdom which Jesus
addressed to those who were disillusioned by the apparent failures of the kingdom to emerge as they had expected. As used here by Mark they serve to inculcate the
correct christian spirit in face of the coming apocalyptic
drama. On the one hand the christian is not to be over-
tense as he awaits Christ's return, for there will be ample
signs for the one who is able to read ordinary indications.
Besides if one is engaged at the task the master has entrusted to him there is no need to fear his return. This
message is very important in the light of the information
that the rest of the section is to give. The moment 'when'
—a very crucial one in Jewish apocalyptic—loses or at
least should lose its urgency for the christian.

*Do you find that the question 'when' still plays too
important a role in christians' lives?*

b and b'. 13 : 30–32. Within this generation, but only the Father knows. These verses indicate Mark's understanding of when the end will come and clearly show that he expects it soon. Already at 9: 1 we find the same note of immediacy, 'within this generation'. At the same time neither Mark, *nor Jesus* can be more specific. In the end the Father will determine when his final gift of himself is to be consummated by bringing about the new creation.

Were Jesus and Mark mistaken in their expectation that the end would come soon? How do you explain this?

c. 13 : 31. The certainty of Jesus' word. Jesus is certain that his words will eventually come true, and it is this note of assurance that Mark wishes to convey to his readers. They are to be consoled with such confidence on Jesus' part, who can call heaven and earth to witness to the truth of his words.

Does the message of Jesus about the future inspire the same confidence for christians today as in Mark's day?

Conclusion : 13 : 37. A final word: 'watch'. The theme of watchfulness or being on one's guard has been expressed in various ways throughout the whole of the discourse and now Mark concludes on this note as the most important message for the christian believer.

7

Scene three: the passion and the glory—the revelation of Sonship
Mk 14:1–16:19

We have now reached the final scene of the drama, and at this stage there is little for Mark to do except allow the full truth about Jesus and his mission to emerge through narrating the facts about these last eventful days. There is an attention to details of place and time in these chapters that one does not find elsewhere in the gospel. At the same time Mark takes care to give us his own interpretation of the events, as we shall see. After the introductory scene of the anointing of Jesus (14:1–11) we are first of all given a secret or sacramental presentation of the climax as Christ's gift of himself to his church and to mankind. This is followed by the public arrest, trial and crucifixion and the dramatic profession of the centurion (15:39). The burial emphasises the reality of the death and the discovery of the empty tomb is a pointer to the final note of the gospel that 'Jesus is risen'. The empty tomb itself does not proclaim this Easter message but poses a question that prepares the disciples for their meeting with the risen Christ and the confirmation of their original hopes that had just been shattered.

Mk 14: 1–11. The anointing at Bethany

Anointing has a special significance in the bible; kings, prophets and priests, for example, are all anointed as a sign of their special dedication to God and the conferring of special power on them. The anointing of Jesus is mentioned at Acts 10: 37 in reference to his baptism, and in the context of his death it means that through his giving of himself Jesus received the kingly power which he claims as his own, through his association with the Son of Man. Jesus is anointed for burial, that is for his death, and the fact that the disciples are indignant at the loss of revenue for 'a good cause' shows how ill prepared they are even now to read the signs of the times. All through the passion story we shall find a similar attitude emerging. Jesus is fulfilling the divine plan on one level, and human agents are judging his actions on a different level, often asking the right question or making a correct observation without any awareness of what they are saying. There is a divine irony about the final scene of the drama, something Jesus indicates now by declaring that this simple act of hospitality and generosity performed in his honour bears within it the seed of the full gospel of his death and resurrection which must be proclaimed everywhere.

1. Indicate situations where the reactions of the disciples to the woman's action would be typical of believers today.

2. What did Jesus mean by declaring that the action of the woman would be told wherever the gospel was preached?

Mk 14: 10–26. The last supper

The whole passion narrative is set in the context of the Jewish passover meal, which celebrated the night of

Israel's liberation from the slavery of Egypt as this was remembered in Jewish tradition beginning with the book of Exodus. Mark sees dramatic irony in the fact that while preparations are going ahead for the Jewish meal (14: 12–16) sinister preparations are afoot to put Jesus to death (14: 1–2; 10–11), thereby bringing about the christian passover which was the fulfilment of its Jewish antecedent. It was not now a question of the liberation of a people from political enslavement, but rather the deliverance of mankind from their sinful situation. As was the case at the entry to Jerusalm earlier, we find one again that everything has been pre-arranged by Jesus, and he is well aware that Judas will betray him. There is a remarkable efficiency about the way Jesus foresees every detail and a remarkable thoroughness about his sense of purpose in going through with it. This is the way in which the early church saw the divine necessity in the death of Jesus, which had been announced as far back as 8: 33, now taking place.

The question whether Jesus celebrated the Jewish passover meal is often discussed. This consisted of an opening blessing followed by a cup of wine passed around of which all partook. Next came the readings from scripture telling the story of the original passover night followed by the singing of the first part of the *Hallel* (Ps 113–118). A second cup was drunk followed by the unleavened bread with bitter herbs. Then the meal proper followed at which the whole paschal lamb was eaten, together with the remaining unleavened bread, which was a reminder to them of the way Yahweh saved their fathers through the blood of a lamb and the haste with which they had to leave Egypt. Next a third cup was passed around together with a prayer of thanksgiving and the ceremony concluded with the singing of the rest of the

Hallel and the final blessing. One can readily see traces
of this meal in the gospel accounts of our Lord's last
supper—the cup of wine, the unleavened bread, the blessing and the singing of the *Hallel*. However only those
elements of the Jewish meal are mentioned which received a new interpretation in the light of the christian
passover. For Mark and the other evangelists the real
significance of the event lies in the eucharistic (thanksgiving) memorial that christians now have of Christ's
death, which was their liberation.

A meal had deep human significance in Israel apart
from the particular religious significance of the paschal
meal. To share one's table with somebody was a sign of
friendship and trust that could not easily be violated.
Consequently the betrayal of Judas is shown up as an act
of outrageous treachery. At the same time, for Jesus himself and for christians subsequently, this meal is a sign
and foretaste of the great meal that was to come with
messianic times. The idea of a feast as a symbol of the
future good times was something that was found repeatedly in Jewish literature and Jesus himself uses it to
describe the kingdom which he preached (Mt 8:11; Lk
14:15–24). When the early christians gathered to celebrate this memorial they reawakened their longing and
expectation for the coming of Christ in glory (cf 1 Cor
11:26) when they would share fully with him in the joy
and fellowship he was now about to enter through his
death (Mk 14:25).

The actual words of institution have a liturgical ring
and probably Mark has preserved them for us in the form
in which they were used by the church of his day. This
would explain the minor variations to be found in the
four different versions of these words that we possess in

the new testament (Mt 26:26–29; Lk 22:15–20; 1 Cor 11:23–25).

When Christ says of the bread 'this is my body' he means 'this is myself', for in Hebrew, as distinct from our Greek-influenced thinking, a man does not *have* a body, but *is* one. The body is not an external clothing that envelops a spiritual soul, the real part of man, but rather it is the whole man as he exists and can communicate with his fellows. In designating the bread as his body Christ is being true to all that we know about himself and his person, which can only be described as a person who wants to give himself to others and to communicate with others at the deepest level possible. The words over the chalice are equally full of meaning. They recall two old testament passages which help us to understand the eucharist at its deepest. The first phrase, 'this is *my* blood of the covenant', recalls Ex 24:8: 'this is *the* blood of the covenant that Yahweh has made with you'. The covenant was God's gift of himself to all Israel to make her his special possession, provided Israel took seriously the words he spoke to her. 'All Israel anwered with one voice, all that the Lord has said to us, we will do, we will obey'. Then the altar and the people were sprinkled with the blood of communion sacrifices to express the life that was shared between Yahweh and his people, for 'the life was in the blood' (Lev 17:11). The second part of Jesus' statement over the chalice echoes the chant of the suffering servant in Isaiah which, we saw, helped Jesus and the early church to understand his death as life-giving on behalf of the sins of the many (cf 10:45). The role of blood in Hebrew sacrifice for sin is not placatory of an angry God, but rather purificatory of a contaminated people (Lev 4 and 16).

This background helps us to understand better the

meaning of Christ's death and its sacramental re-enact-
ment in the eucharist. It is the act by which God gives
himself and his life most completely, in his new covenant
or self-giving (Jer 31:31 ff). Despite our sins which disrupt such relationship we share as a people together ('all
Israel answered with *one* voice') in the divine self-giving
that has reached its climax in and through the death of
Jesus.

*1. How could the eucharist retain for us the sense of
expectation of messianic blessings which it had for early
christians?*

*2. How has the old testament background helped you to
understand better the eucharist as a community celebration?*

*3. The new testament emphasis on the saving quality
of the blood of Christ can only be understood properly
against the background of blood in Israel's sacrifices.
Discuss this.*

Mk 14:26–42. The agony in the garden

This passage is introduced by Peter's confident assurance
that he would never betray Jesus, even though they have
all been warned that they will fall away (literally 'be
scandalised') because of what is about to happen to him
their shepherd. Earlier at 6:32 Jesus had compassion on
the crowd who were like sheep without a shepherd. Now
however, those of the crowd who have followed, namely
the disciples, are in danger of finding the treatment of the
shepherd scandalous. Their following of him must be
fully purified. Peter is no longer Satan, obstructing the
way of God for Jesus, but he is confident in his own ability

to meet any eventuality. At least his heart is in the right place, which is more than could be said for the callous Judas. Jesus speaks of his resurrection and of meeting them again in Galilee, but so intent are Peter and the others on protesting their generosity that the idea of resurrection does not even register with them, if only to query it. Yet this mention of Galilee, the place of their original vocation 'to be with Jesus' and 'to be sent' will come back to them at a crucial point later.

The agony of Jesus is the most 'shocking' event in the gospel in that it brings home to us the real humanity of Jesus, despite his willing and complete acceptance of his chalice long before this (Mk 10:38). His prayer is not an attempt to escape, but rather a desire that God's kingdom (his will) might manifest itself now to humanity in a way other than through this chalice. His request to his disciples 'to watch' recalls his advice to all in Mk 13 to be ready for the eschatological drama, and his prayer to God as 'Abba' shows that despite the demands of the moment, God is still for him goodness, care, love itself, who can only be addressed as Father. For the first time since his election and reception of a new name (3:16) Peter is called by his old name Simon, something that corresponds with his present inadequacy to remain awake, that is actively participate in the events about to take place. Jesus is faced with 'the hour' of the eschatological drama, yet Peter cannot watch one hour. Jesus prays when the moment appears too much for him, and, as earlier at 1:35 and 6:46, he discovers the strength to go ahead to meet his enemies and give himself positively to God's will.

What do you learn about human nature and christian response from the attitude of the disciples here?

Mk 14:43–51. The arrest

In these few verses Mark paints a picture of various reactions to what was a highly tense and dramatic situation.
The mob is armed with all kinds of equipment to deal
with a violent insurrection. Judas on the other hand be-
haves like the two-faced person he has shown himself to
be, giving Jesus a kiss, the usual form of friendly greeting
among orientals. The reaction of the disciples is typical
also—a brave exterior display that misunderstands the
whole situation, and in the end all of them desert Jesus.
He alone is true and sincere to his original commitment.
The scriptures must be fulfilled, that is, God's will must
be accomplished, and so he does not resist his arrest. It is
the soldiers who are afraid, not Jesus. Finally Mark has
another actor in this grim scene, the young man who followed him, but who got away naked as he was about to be
seized. Many suggestions have been put forward about
the identity of the young man but without any agreement. It may well be a veiled reference to Mark himself
as an authentication of the story he is telling. The early
christians at Jerusalem met to celebrate the eucharist at
the house of the mother of John Mark (Acts 12:12). Accordingly, the suggestion has been made that the upper
room where Christ celebrated the last supper was there
also, and that this young man, John Mark, who is identified with the writer of the gospel, was prompted to attach
himself to Jesus and his retinue quite unnoticed, and so
was an actual eye-witness of the events narrated. At all
events he serves here as a remarkable contrast to the disciples who fled for fear of being captured.

*How does this description of reactions to Jesus corre-
spond to what one finds among christians today?*

Mk 14:53–72. The trial before the sanhedrin and Peter's denial

Peter protested that he would die with Christ rather than deny him and now the evangelist weaves the story of Peter's denial into the narrative of Jesus' trial. It serves to fill out the human situation for us as we await the dawn when the due process of law can be carried out by obtaining a conviction from the Roman governor. Peter shows himself to be the same human Peter that we have come to know in the gospel, generous and impetuous in his reactions, yet human and selfish in his appraisal of situations when danger threatens.

The trial before the sanhedrin seems to have been a preliminary investigation, since at 15:1 we hear of a morning consultation before they took Jesus to Pilate. The scene centres around the witness brought against Jesus, which Mark emphasises twice was *false* witness, and the reply of Jesus to the high priest's question, 'are you the Christ?' Both refer to two signs that Jesus gives of the new age about to be inaugurated.

The false witness concerns Jesus and the temple. As a prelude to the passion Jesus had driven the money changers from the temple, declaring it a house of prayer *for all nations* (11:15–19) and later at 13:1 ff we have seen how his prophecy of the destruction of the temple was made in the context of the glorious return of the Son of Man. Jesus was interested in both the destruction and remaking of the temple and yet the testimony of the witnesses was false for Mark because they thought Jesus was speaking about the temple of Solomon at Jerusalem when in fact he was talking of a temple 'not made with hands', a description which Mark alone of the evangelists gives, that is 'not of this creation', as the epistle to the Hebrews puts it so aptly (Heb 9:2). Thus while they spoke the truth their witness was false because they had totally misunderstood the purpose and meaning of Jesus in regard to the temple, and had failed to understand the connection with the risen body of Christ, the new dwelling place of God with men, that is achieved through the death of Jesus. Thus in a wholly unexpected way the temple prophecy is realised in Jesus' death and resurrection and all have now access to God in one body, Jew and Greek, slave and free (Gal 3:28). That is why Mark tells us that with the death of Jesus 'the veil of the temple was rent in two from top to bottom' (15:38). The metaphor of the temple, the traditional place of God's dwelling with his people, is very suitable to describe the new reality of grace that God has made available to man in Christ. Mark has cleverly interwoven this theology of the new temple into his apparently factual narrative of the passion, thereby giving us a deep insight into the meaning and significance of Christ's death.

The second sign that Jesus gives is that of the Son of Man sitting on the right hand of Power and coming on the clouds of heaven. Once again Mark makes opponents of Jesus a spokesman for the true understanding of his person, something that helps to bring out the real irony of the situation. The high priest asks, 'Are you the Christ the Son of the Blessed?' We have already seen that for Mark the title 'the Christ' is only a stage on the way to a true understanding of Jesus, and here we see this title being filled out by Mark's favourite one 'Son of God' (or the Blessed). Jesus replies in the affirmative, thus breaking his silence for the first time in the gospel. But his reply indicates that this is something yet to emerge. 'You *will* see.' Seeing has been a favourite metaphor of Mark's to indicate the vision of faith that understands Jesus and his

mission, and faith will again be required before his true
dignity will be recognised. Jesus' reply consists of combining two old testament texts, Ps 110:2 and Dan 7:13,
to describe his future status, and this leads to his being
accused of blasphemy. The first text referred to the enthronement of a king and the special place of honour with
Yahweh that was his as a son of David. It referred to a
this-world messiah, therefore. The reference to the Son of
Man on the other hand introduces an other-world figure
who shares a mysterious origin with God. By combining
these two figures of Jewish expectation the picture of each
is filled out. The glorious Son of Man is a figure of this
world, while the dignity of the son of David and his
authority is no longer symbolic but real since it is a share
in the very authority of God. Jesus' messiahship is not
that of a political figure who could be called son of God
in the way that kings and even Israel itself were called
by that title in the old testament. His sonship is of a
different order. Little wonder he is accused of blasphemy.

*1. Does Peter's denial make the church less credible
today?*

*2. How does the idea of the temple help you to under-
stand the death of Christ and its value?*

Mk 15:1–20. The Roman trial

The Roman trial concerns 'the king of the Jews', a title
that is used four times in this section, 15:2, 8, 12, 18. This
may have had an apologetic purpose in the Rome of
Mark's day. 'King of the Jews' could well have been an
inflammatory title for Jesus and might have been used to
discredit the christians at Rome as bad citizens who refused to worship the emperor. At all events Mark makes

it clear that Jesus had no political pretensions despite the title. Rather Barabbas who was released in his place is described by Mark as one of the rebels who had 'committed murder in an insurrection'. Neither did Pilate issue a formal sentence against Jesus but handed him over to be crucified in order to placate the excited mob, even though he knew it was through envy that they had brought Jesus before him. The silence of Jesus and the subsequent mockery by the soldiers reminds us of the insults that the suffering servant was treated with according to Is 53. At his hour of agony Jesus too is silent before his persecutors.

1. How should the attitude of Jesus before Pilate and his tormentors help christians to understand their vocation?

2. What are the political dangers for christians who follow Jesus today and how should they try to face them?

Mk 15:21–39. The crucifixion and death of Jesus

The manner of Jesus' death—crucifixion—and the fact that he was bracketed with two robbers is an indication of the way in which he was regarded by the crowd, so successful had the propaganda of the chief priests been in inciting an inquisitive and kindly, if unsuspecting, crowd to open hostility against him. Jesus refuses any palliative now, nothing will prevent him from drinking the chalice that his Father is offering him. The bystanders are said by Mark to blaspheme Jesus (15:29), which was earlier said of those who denied the true source of Jesus' victory over Satan, the Spirit of God (3:28 f). Jesus had been condemned as guilty of blasphemy because he declared his own true dignity at 14:66, but in fact it is they who are the real blasphemers, Mark comments. Their earlier

blasphemy in not recognising the true source of Jesus'
power, attributing it to Satan, is now matched by their
failure to recognise him. Instead they looked for a
miraculous manifestation of his power, that 'they may
see and believe'. They have refused to see or believe,
despite all the signs Jesus has performed, yet now they
declare themselves willing if Jesus will give a startling
display of power. However, all along Jesus has refused
such requests, as being typical of false Christs (13:21 f)
and has explicitly condemned such an attitude at 8:11–
13. Now as he gives the greatest sign of his love he is not
likely to succumb to this human temptation that has been
put in his way by his enemies who are really Satan's agents
in human guise. In the early part of the gospel the
demoniacs always addressed Jesus by his correct title
without any acceptance of what such titles implied. At
that point Jesus reacted by imposing silence on them.
Now his human enemies adopt the same ploy; the high
priest (14:61) and the scribes use correct titles for Jesus
in blasphemous mockery but now he is silent before
them.

The actual death of Jesus has all the appearances of a
terrifying and terrible event. Twice Mark reports that
Jesus 'cried with a loud voice', a description he uses
earlier for the departing demons (5:7; 9:26). This gives
a demonic atmosphere to the scene and the darkness that
surrounds the events only helps to heighten this effect—
it is as though the power of evil has taken over completely.
The cry of Jesus is not the despairing histrionics of an expelled demon, however, but a confident plea to his God
and Father (see the whole of Ps 22), a cry that will shortly
be vindicated by his resurrection. Thus as Jesus dies, suddenly the veil of the temple is rent in two to fulfil the first
sign Mark had given during the trial before the san-

hedrin. The veil that separated the sanctuary from the outer courts and rendered it inaccessible to all except the high priest, and he only once a year, has now no further meaning. The death of Jesus has suddenly and dramatically opened the way to God for all.

The second sign from the scene with the sanhedrin is also realised now—the full dignity of Jesus is startingly revealed and recognised in and through his death. Jesus had said to the high priest 'You will *see*' and now the centurion, a simple Roman officer performing his duty, not an arrogant Jewish religious leader, *saw* and *believed*: 'Truly this man was Son of God'. At the opening verse of the gospel the evangelist had revealed its content to the reader, namely that Jesus was the Son of God. However, subsequent events were to show that this was a vocation for Jesus rather than a title of honour. In particular it was a vocation for him to show himself as the well-beloved Son, that is as the new Isaac who, according to Jewish tradition, freely gave his life so that the blessing of Yahweh might pass to posterity. Jesus has now done this willingly and freely and so the mountain of sacrifice, Jerusalem, the city of Yahweh's temple, becomes the mountain of revelation where Yahweh's new temple will be fashioned for all the nations to adore. Only now does a human being recognise the true dignity of Jesus and make a genuine confession of faith in the full message of the gospel. God is no longer hidden behind the veil, but the extent of his love in giving his well-beloved Son to death lies open to those who have eyes to see (Rom 5: 1–11). Only now may Jesus be openly proclaimed and so the secrecy motif has finally come to an end. Significantly for Mark and his readers, it was a Roman who first makes this breakthrough at the paradoxical moment of Jesus' apparent rejection by God as a lawless man.

1. Explain why the death of Jesus reveals his true dignity.

2. Why was the centurion able to believe, whereas the religious leaders' hearts remained closed?

3. How did Jesus overcome the powers of evil by his death?

Mk 15:40–47. The burial of Jesus

Pointedly, Mark mentions others besides the centurion who stood beside the cross; namely the women who had followed Jesus from Galilee. Strangely Mark does not mention Mary, the mother of Jesus, at this point, though John's gospel gives her a very prominent place at the foot of the cross. The women are the witnesses to the actual burial of Jesus, and so are in a position to be at the tomb to hear the Easter message (15:47; 16:1 ff). The actual narrative of the burial is meant to emphasise the reality of the death of Jesus and the fact that the tomb can be associated with a particular individual shows how important a datum this was for the early church's belief in the resurrection. Joseph of Arimathea as a member of the sanhedrin would have taken part in the abortive trial that arranged for the death of Jesus, but now that the deed is done he who was sincerely searching for the kingdom, and presumably was attracted to Jesus, discovers his courage and openly arranges for the burial. There is no trace of a disciple at this sad moment and not even Peter is around to witness the end. The women, however, prepare to pay the last homage of proper burial to Jesus once the sabbath is over.

Is there any special significance to the fact that the women were loyal to Jesus?

Mk 16:1–8. The empty tomb

This is the final scene of Mark's gospel as we now have it and it has been well prepared for already. The fact that it is the women who first discover the empty tomb shows how authentic the basic fact must be since women were not recognised as official witnesses at the time. Not only are they the ones to discover the tomb, they are also the ones to receive the message that Jesus is risen and has gone before Peter and the disciples to Galilee, as he promised (14:28). Jesus led the disciples from Galilee to Jerusalem, but now they must find their way back there to meet their risen Lord. They no longer have the physical presence of the master to prop up their weak and faltering faith. Instead, they are challenged to question all their old presuppositions and disillusionment with Jesus by the discovery of the empty tomb. They must launch out again in search of the master, no longer lured by his presence but challenged by his promise and the word of his messenger, whose description (seated at the right side and dressed in white) is a hint for them of the true status of Jesus seated at the right hand of Power (14:62) and 'glistening in white garments such as no fuller *on earth* could bleach them' (9:3). Once they meet their risen Lord all they had experienced in Galilee with him will suddenly be clarified and they will be able to relate these experiences to the world. For the moment though a discreet silence must be maintained.

1. What part did the empty tomb play in the faith of the women and the disciples regarding the resurrection of Jesus?

2. Why were the disciples ordered to return to Galilee?

Mk 16:9–19. Epilogue: preach the gospel to every creature

The prologue to the gospel told us that it concerned Jesus Christ, the Son of God. Now the story has been fully unfolded, and the truth of that gospel has been manifested : Jesus, the crucified one, is risen, is the Easter message that can be proclaimed. It is only when that is fully understood that genuine faith in Jesus as Son of God is possible. In all probability Mark's gospel originally ended with an appearance of the risen Christ and a command to preach the gospel. However, for some reason that ending has been lost from the manuscripts and 16:9–19 is a later ending which is really a summary of post-resurrection accounts from Luke's and Matthew's gospels, and presumably is later than both of those gospels. The central idea is that the risen Christ who has now had his claims as the glorious Son of Man who had first to suffer vindicated by his Father can issue his command to preach the gospel to every creature. As the risen one he is freed from the limitations of time and space and present wherever his gospel is preached and his way followed. The community which believes in such a presence must continue his struggle against every manifestation of evil, and proclaim his gospel everywhere until he comes, since it is a message that vitally concerns every man.

Why is the commission to preach the gospel on a universal basis only given after the resurrection?

Matthew

Henry Wansbrough

1

The prelude
Mt 1:1–2:23

Mt 1:1–25. Jesus' ancestry

The gospel of Mark, which lay before Matthew as he wrote, began with the manifestation of Jesus at his baptism. For Matthew this was not enough; he wanted to show that Jesus may be seen to be the messiah even in the stories of his birth and infancy. Where he derived these stories from it is hard to see, for it is notable that Mark shows no trace of them and Luke shares with them only the most basic facts. No doubt Matthew is working on some data of the christian tradition, but his overriding concern is to bring out the meaning of Jesus' birth and infancy by showing how God's hand was at work in these events. For this purpose he relates the stories in a way familiar in Jewish writing, showing the meaning of the events by drawing attention, not by editorial comment but by the very way he tells the story, to parallel events in the old testament and in Jewish tradition. Occasionally he actually quotes the scripture to which he is referring, but more often throughout his gospel he merely alludes to it, leaving a reader steeped in the old testament to appreciate the allusion.

All the evangelists are Jewish in mentality, but Matthew most of all. The evangelists are concerned primarily to show that Jesus was the messiah awaited by the Jews,

who was to restore all things to their former paradisiac
state, to bring God's rule to fulfilment on earth, to bring
into being an ideal kingdom of bliss and plenty. This
task was not easy, for the Jews' expectation was pretty
material: they took for granted that the messianic revolution would throw off the hated yoke of the Romans and
establish a world-empire of the Jews. They were orientals,
and their picture of bliss and plenty did not stop at
expectations of perpetual banqueting without any toil
under the hot sun. Jesus therefore, and the evangelists
after him, were confronted with the dual task of showing
that he was this expected messiah and that the renewal of
all things which he brought was not quite as they had
expected it. It was the refusal of the majority of Jews to
throw away their preconceptions and adapt to the unexpected reality which led to the crucifixion.

Matthew's first task, then, is to show that Jesus was the
messiah. One of the dominant points in the expectation
of the messiah was that he should be of the line of David,
for David had been the ideal king of the united kingdom
of Israel and Judah, to whom the Jews still looked back
with longing. The Lord had promised both that David's
kingly line would never end and that his own representative who was to establish a state of idyllic peace on earth
would be a second David. But here immediately a difficulty confronts the evangelist, for Jesus was born of a
virgin, and so had no father through whom he could be
heir to the line of David. (Succession through the female
line was a highly dubious concept, and anyway there is
no evidence that Mary was of the line of David.) Jesus
then belonged to the line of David through Joseph, his
adoptive father.

This is the reason why Matthew opens his gospel with
a long genealogy of Joseph, not one of Mary. The gene-

alogy itself is highly stylised, omitting a vast number of generations and intent on showing little more than Joseph's quality of son of David and son of Abraham, uninterested in the intervening stages, which are merely grouped in functions of the perfect number seven in the classic three periods of history: Abraham to David, David to the exile at Babylon, the exile to Christ. There is one significant detail: the women. Each of the four women mentioned (Tamar, Rahab, Ruth, Bethsheba) joined the line of Abraham through some extraordinary circumstance; Matthew is preparing for the fact that Jesus' birth from Mary and incorporation into the line of David will be similarly accompanied by extraordinary circumstances.

The purpose of the genealogy is made clear by its completion in the story of the adoption of Jesus into the house of David. This is only incidentally the story of the birth of Jesus or of the virginal conception by Mary. The point of it is made clear both by its position after the genealogy and by its climax in the final punch-line 'and he called his name Jesus', for naming was the act by which a father acknowledged the son as his own, or—in this case —adopted him as his own.

In telling the story Matthew has two main preoccupations: first he wants to answer the question, how did Joseph dare meddle in the matter, knowing that the child was conceived miraculously without any human father? At the same time he wants to show that Jesus' adoption into the house of David was no chance occurrence but was carefully engineered by God. It is Joseph's awareness of the impropriety of his continuing with the marriage to Mary in view of what has happened which occasions the dream in the first place. There is no question of his suspecting her of adultery (although their marriage was not

yet complete, a Jewish engagement had many of the qualities of a modern marriage, and getting a child by another
man would rank as adultery). If this had been the case he
would have been bound to denounce her rather than 'put
her away secretly' out of misplaced soft-heartedness. The
narrative makes altogether better sense if Joseph was well
aware how the child had been conceived, and needed the
angel's message not to tell him this but to inform him that
in spite of this it was God's command that he should make
the child his own, and so incorporate him into the house
of David by himself giving the child a name. As always
in judaism the name itself augurs the role of the child
who bears it.

*1. What is the point of Jesus being born of a virgin? Is
it because of a fear of sex as sinful?*

*2. Why this insistence of Matthew on presenting Jesus
as the messiah? Can't we break away from the Jewish
concepts of our faith into more modern ones?*

Mt 2:1–23. Flight into Egypt

Matthew relates only a single incident in Jesus' life before
the baptism, so that we may suppose that it is chosen with
special care and has special importance. Its special character is shown also by the fact that all but one of the four
scenes of which it is composed is conducted under the
special guidance of God, either by the star or by the word
of an angel. Only Herod's massacre of the babies is—for
obvious reasons—not so guided. But, even so, this scene
as well is under God's special providence, for Matthew is
careful to note that it too fulfils the scripture. Matthew
regularly points out that Jesus is, in this or that way, fulfilling the scriptures—or even that he acts in a certain

way in order to fulfil the scriptures—on occasions when we would consider the sense of the quotation given to be extremely forced.

Jewish exegesis of the scripture at this time was extremely literal. It was considered wholly legitimate to fasten on one word and interpret it quite apart from its context. This attitude originated in an exaggerated respect for every letter of scripture and a determination to find as much richness of doctrine in each of them as possible. In the same way Matthew, rightly convinced that all the scriptures speak of Christ, expresses this conviction by suggesting a one-to-one correspondence between the individual events of Jesus' life and scriptural texts; it is in fact more the whole movement of the old testament which breathes Christ than the individual texts.

What particular significance did Matthew see in this incident of the flight into Egypt that he should so single it out from all the others of Jesus' childhood? From the way he tells the story, it is clear that he sees Jesus in this story as the second Moses. This is again in accord with Jewish expectation of the messiah, for he was to fulfil Moses' own prophecy: 'Yahweh your God will raise up for you a prophet like myself' (Deut 18:15). As Moses had founded the old people of God and led them to freedom, so Jesus was to found a new people and lead them to a new kingdom. This thought recurs constantly, though allusively, in Matthew, particularly in the theme of a new people composed of gentile as well as Jew which will replace the old chosen people.

That Jesus is the prophesied second Moses is shown by the detailed correspondence of the story in Mt 2 with the story of Moses before the exodus, as told by a combination of the bible and Jewish tradition. At Moses' birth the king of Egypt dreamt that one had been born who was to supplant him; at this the whole city was troubled (as Jerusalem in 2:3) and the king consulted his wise men and astrologers (as Herod in 2:4). They advised him to kill all the male children, which he attempted to do, without attaining the new 'king' (as Herod in 2:16). At a later date Moses was compelled to flee from the land of his birth (as the holy family in 2:14); he stays in exile until he receives a divine message to return home 'for all those who wanted to kill you are dead' (Ex 4:19, whose wording is identical to Mt 2:20). Thus Matthew combines two different stories about Moses to describe the journey of the holy family. In the second, of course, the place-names must be adjusted, for Moses fled from Egypt while Jesus fled from Palestine to Egypt.

The question immediately arises whether Matthew invented this event in Jesus' life simply in order to illustrate that Jesus was the second Moses. There is certainly nothing impossible in the story, for Egypt is no further from Bethlehem than Nazareth is, and Herod was a bloodthirsty tyrant whose insane suspicions of possible rivals made him put numbers of his closest relatives to death; he would hardly baulk at the few male children produced in two years in a little village in the hills. The only puzzle is how Matthew came to know this eminently suitable story. His only sources for his gospel appear to be Mark's gospel and a collection of the sayings of Jesus (which he shares with Luke). While he could have derived from the general christian knowledge of Jesus that he was born of a virgin at Bethlehem, it is unlikely that just this one story of the flight into Egypt came down to him through the channels of the tradition. It would certainly be consonant with Jewish literary conventions for Matthew to have embroidered the journey from Bethlehem to Nazareth in such a way as to bring out that even at this stage

Jesus was the messiah and the new Moses. But certainty on this point is impossible—and unnecessary.

One element in the story has been neglected so far: the magi and their star. The three kings have come to play such a large part in the christian imagination that it comes as a shock to learn that in the text they were neither three nor kings, but simply an unspecified number of wise men or magicians from east of Palestine, the traditional home of wise men in Jewish lore. Astrology and spells were much practised in Palestine at this time, in spite of religious prohibitions, and it may well be that their gifts to Jesus represent the submission to Christ of the occult sciences. As for the star, it is scarcely necessary to look for a comet with which this may be identified, for the appearance of a star at the birth of a great man is frequently claimed both within and especially outside Jewish literature. It is a sign, then, that a great man has been born.

1. In what ways does the old testament testify to Christ?

2. Does it matter whether the 'flight into Egypt' was actually into Egypt? Can the resurrection be treated in the same way?

2

Jesus appears in public
Mt 3:1–4:24

The gospel begins at this point, for the baptism of Jesus was always one of the central points of christian preaching, since it was then that Jesus' messianic mission began, his church began to take shape. What preceded had only been introduction and preparation. The main body of Matthew's gospel (chapters 3 to 25) falls into five 'books', each of which contains a narrative section and a discourse or sermon formed from a collection of Jesus' teaching on a particular subject. The first book consists of Jesus' first public appearances and the sermon on the mount, which gives teaching about the basic conduct of any of his followers.

Mt 3:1–12. Jesus is proclaimed messiah
John the Baptist now comes on the scene. He is a figure in the line of the old testament prophets whose function is twofold: to shock the people into a realisation that the time for a total renewal has come, and to point to Jesus who brings this renewal. It was immediately obvious from his bizarre clothing that he claimed to be a prophet, for both the garment of hair and a leather loin-cloth are distinctive marks of the prophet in the old testament.

John's role as a prophet was to provide a setting for the

146

opening of Jesus' mission. His message is revolution, to shake people out of their comfortable mediocrity by bringing home to them that the promised time of renewal has come, and so to form a community ready to receive the imminent breaking-in of the new state of things. The emphasis of his message is very different from that of Jesus, sterner, and concentrating more on the cataclysmic and destructive nature of the event for those who refuse to receive the messiah, whereas Jesus concentrates on the love extended to all who are willing to respond to it. Because of this dual potential the confrontation with Jesus at his first coming constitutes a judgement in the same way as the meeting with him at the final coming. The Baptist, however, is so filled with the old testament idea that the day of the Lord's coming will be essentially a *dies irae* that he will later be led by Jesus' actions of kindness and mercy to doubt temporarily whether he is really the promised messiah.

Positively about the messiah he says little: he surpasses John infinitely in power and dignity, for John is not worthy to carry his sandals; this was the most menial of tasks, so menial that it might not be imposed on a Jewish slave, and yet John is unworthy of it. And Jesus will baptise with the spirit and with fire; these are two elements prophesied for the last times of the messiah. The first is a refining fire which would purge away all the base metal in God's people, leaving a pure and tempered metal, tried and tested in the furnace, for God. The spirit is the new spirit which Ezekiel had promised that God would breathe into his people, making them a new creation with a new life, and a new heart sensitive to the promptings of his inspiration and his love.

1. What is the relevance of all this about John and the precursor of the messiah to modern times?

2. Do we find today the church closer to John the Baptist's system of ideas or to Jesus Christ's?

Mt 3:13–17. Jesus is baptised

The first great problem here is: why did Jesus need to be baptised? This was a difficulty felt by the early christians, for Matthew inserts into the narrative the little dialogue about this between John and Jesus. It is supposed to answer the question, but 'to achieve all righteousness' remains enigmatic enough. Since 'achieve' or 'fulfil' is often used by Matthew in the sense of perfecting or bringing to completion the old dispensation, a possible sense of Jesus' saying is that by submitting to baptism he shows that he is entering the community formed to receive the messiah, and by so doing bringing the old dispensation (whose whole sense was looking towards the messiah) to its predestined conclusion.

But more important than the baptism itself are the descent of the Spirit and the divine witness. Whatever physical form these may have taken they clearly constitute a decisive moment for Jesus' human psychology. Though he was God he was also man, and as man learnt and developed like other men, though of course endowed with unparalleled powers of insight and perception. The moment when he comes up from the baptism is the moment when he receives the divine message that his messianic mission is to start. The evangelist's wording shows that he at least—and surely Jesus before him—saw the descent of the Spirit as fulfilling the prophecies of Isaiah (42:1; 61:1) that the Spirit of the Lord would come down on his servant for his mission to bring justice to the nations and inaugurate the renewal of the world. The voice from heaven too perhaps has resonances of the same prophecies of the servant of the Lord, for it has been surmised that the original Aramaic read: 'Here is my servant, my chosen one in whom my soul delights' as Is 42:1, the opening lines of the prophecy. In any case the Spirit of God is always given for a mission, giving power to perform a service in God's people; this is the meaning of the descent of the Spirit upon Jesus.

1. What is this Holy Spirit like? Did he give Jesus the kind of power that spiritualist mediums have? Where do we find the Spirit among people nowadays? Do we need the Spirit?

2. How has justice come down on the nations? If Jesus fulfilled this prophecy presumably justice is here now for all people—but where is it? Look at the suffering of the world; look at our indifference to its suffering in the West.

Mt 4:1–11. Temptation in the desert

After Jesus has received the divine indication that his mission is to start he is led by God's own Spirit to be tested. At first sight this seems strange; but in late judaism testing (or tempting, the word is the same) came to be regarded as a privilege and mark of God's favour. Clearly, he who survives the trial emerges strengthened and purified.

In Jesus' case this testing can be viewed on two levels, one scriptural and one psychological. The account is very closely modelled on the story of the testing of Israel in the desert after the exodus. Expressions drawn from this story reappear several times, and notably Jesus' replies are each time couched in words from the book of Deuteronomy regarding that testing. The lesson is that, where

Israel was tested and failed, Jesus, who has just been seen
as the head of the new Israel, remains faithful.

At the psychological level we can learn much of Jesus
from this story. It is already clear that the story is stylised;
but the basis remains that Jesus was pulled in various
ways by the devil away from the path laid down for him
by God. It is highly plausible that after the sign to start
his mission he should, under divine guidance, retire for a
period of preparation (forty days is a standard biblical
figure for a longish period of preparation, especially accompanied by fasting), during which he works out the
exact modality of his messianic mission. Among the various ways in which it was expected that the messiah should
come many had a superficial attractiveness; but they are
rejected as being the devil's ways, not God's, and Jesus
returns to the one way already laid before him, the way
of suffering according to the model of the suffering servant of the Lord in Isaiah's prophecy.

The first temptation, symbolised by the bread, is to
bring a new era of physical abundance, plenty of food and
banqueting, according to the coarsest of the versions of
the Jewish messianic hope. The second is to show his messianic dignity irrefutably by a dramatic sign—a personal
public display such as the disciples begged him to do in
John 7, but incompatible with his way of tact and rejection. The third temptation is to political messiahship,
to found a world empire, according to the hopes of that
party of the Jews who longed to turn the tables on their
oppressors, the Romans. But this embrace of wordly
power is the worst of all, and would be worship of the
devil himself.

In this third temptation a scriptural theme found already in chapter 2 reappears: Jesus is the new Moses. For
Moses too was taken to the top of a high mountain and

shown all the land which his descendants would rule. Only the land offered to Jesus is even greater (all the land shown to Moses is not really quite visible from the top of any real mountain; when all the kingdoms of the world are shown to Jesus, the author is using the same figure of speech, though slightly extended).

1. Why should Christ have to follow this way of suffering and rejection? Why could he not both reject the devil and remain faithful to God—and so be successful?

2. May we legitimately deduce anything from the third temptation about a christian's attitude to politics?

Mt 4:12-24. Early activity in Galilee

Jesus now returns to Galilee and begins his mission of teaching and of showing by his healing activity that the messianic times have come. He proclaims not that he, the messiah, has come, but that the kingdom of heaven has drawn near. This kingdom of heaven—really 'of God', for 'of heaven' is merely a reverent Jewish way of avoiding use of the divine name—will be the central object of his preaching; at first mysterious, its meaning gradually unfolds. In one sense it has already come in Jesus; yet his followers can still pray that it should come, for it is not yet fully achieved. It is a thing of power, yet weak; it is proclaimed, yet unrecognised. It is no territorial kingdom but within men, and yet linked to a visible community. It is God's complete rule over men, yet the members of the kingdom include bad fish as well as good. It is the renewal of all things which the messiah was to bring, yet so little seems to be changed by it. As the kingdom is the first object of Jesus' teaching, so it is in many ways the centre, a many-sided entity in which understanding of many elements in christianity is bound up.

The most noticeable characteristic of this first activity of Jesus is that he immediately starts to form a community. The kingdom is not in or for himself alone, but is of and for men. From the call of the first disciples we already learn something of the nature of the kingdom, especially since this narrative makes no attempt to seem true to life (was this their first meeting with Jesus? Did he not say for what purpose they were to follow?), but is an example of a schematic type of narrative which occurs several times in the gospel, filed down to its theological essentials. Discipleship of Jesus consists in following him, in response to his call (those who offer themselves are turned away). The response must be immediate, 'at once', and total: 'leaving their nets . . . the boat and their father'. The demands of the kingdom are absolute.

To what extent do we in the church today have our views about how we should follow Christ? Do we give unconditional service? Is the important thing to follow Christ? Or to follow an ideal? A person? Or human aspirations?

3
The sermon on the mount
Mt 5:1–7:29

Mt 5:1–12. The beatitudes
Of the five great collections of sayings of Jesus given by
Matthew each methodically deals with one aspect of the
Lord's teaching. He is far more systematic than Mark or
Luke, and takes different sayings on related subjects from
all available sources to assemble them in a complete treatment of each matter. So the first collection gives teaching
on the basic conditions of membership of the kingdom
and so constitutes a sort of preliminary manifesto of the
kingdom.

The opening of the manifesto proclaims in a series of
monumental statements who are the members of the kingdom—'for theirs is the kingdom of heaven' end the first
and the last of the beatitudes. To a pious Jew this series
of hard-hitting statements would have been scandalous :
nothing about descent from Abraham? Nothing about
observing the law, paying tithes, avoiding contact with
the unclean, keeping the sabbath? If anything, Luke's
more primitive version is still more hard-hitting and
would have been still more scandalous. For Matthew expands and explains a little, teaching what a follower of
Jesus must do. But Luke's is more a proclamation that
the kingdom belongs to the misfits and outcasts of society:

Blessed are you who are poor: yours is the kingdom of
    God;
blessed are you who are hungry now: you shall be
    satisfied;
blessed are you who weep now: you shall laugh;
blessed are you when people hate you, drive you out,
    abuse you.   [Lk 6: 20–22]

And there follows a condemnation of the rich, contented
and successful, who want for nothing and therefore do not
seek the kingdom. Luke's message is addressd to those
despised and rejected by the so-called religious leaders of
Israel. But Matthew's message is more general: the conditions required for being a member. He explains that mere
poverty is not enough; there must be an attitude of mind
and a hunger not merely for food but for 'what is right';
his first four beatitudes put forward an attitude of openness and receptiveness, consciousness of inadequacy and
need of help. Then Matthew adds three beatitudes which
demand good works, showing—as he often stresses in his
gospel—that love is shown for God principally by love
of neighbour. Mercy is best defined as that quality for
lack of which the hard and censorious Pharisees were
condemned. Peace, always the normal Jewish greeting,
becomes the special keynote of christians, the song of
angels at Bethlehem, the content of the gospel which the
disciples are sent out to preach and the chief blessing
Paul invokes in his letters; hence the blessedness of peace-
makers.

*1. How is a christian to remain pure in heart in our
society that is among other things so sex-conscious?*

2. Do we have to seek persecution to be a true christian?

3. Is it our job always to seek out injustice and try to

cure it, so making ourselves unpopular in 'respectable society'? How does an attitude towards injustice, which might cause real trouble, eg if one attacks a rich minority in a poor country, square with the beatitude about peace-making?

Mt 5 : 13–48. Perfecting the old law

After two short series of collected sayings about the missionary task of christians as the salt of the earth and the light of the world by their good example, Matthew gives an example of how Jesus brings the old dispensation to its perfection. This is a theme which runs through his gospel, and is here applied to Jesus' teaching on the moral law, by a series of six antitheses between the requirements of the old law and the more demanding requirements of Christ.

The way the teaching is put forward is typically Jewish, in two ways: firstly, he begins with a general principle 'if your virtue goes no deeper than that of the scribes and Pharisees . . .' and follows with a number of applications of it; in rabbinic terminology, these are called respectively 'ancestor' and 'descendants'. Secondly, 'you have heard how it was said' is a typical formula for a usual interpretation which was to be corrected; the only difference is significant: the rabbis never put forward a new interpretation on their own authority but always relied on some traditional authority. But Jesus precisely reverses this, boldly opposing his own to the authority of tradition: 'but *I* say this to you'; it was this which awed his listeners 'because he taught them with authority, not as their own scribes' (7 : 29). This is not to say that Jesus himself gave all these teachings on one occasion, or even necessarily in this form; for instance Matthew clearly excerpts the teaching on divorce from the story of an incident which he relates in 19:1–9. He gathers examples to illustrate the 'ancestor' which stands at the head of the section.

The demands of these antitheses cover various matters, but all stand under the sign of more perfect love of one's neighbour. The first considers actions which express lack of love, and the last stresses the universal extent of love which is required of Christ's followers. This was especially striking to Jews, who were obliged to treat as neighbours only fellow-Jews and even considered it a duty to regard all others as pariahs; the extension of love to all men was Jesus' own innovation. It is the backbone of all Matthew's moral counsels: it sums up all the commandments after love of God, it is for lack of this that the scribes and Pharisees are condemned, it is on this point exclusively that men are divided at the last judgement. It is to this perfection, therefore, that Matthew refers when he concludes: 'You must therefore be perfect just as your heavenly Father is perfect.'

1. How seriously should we take these counsels on anger, and impurity in one's heart against another? Is it not impossible to avoid these two faults?

2. How does one square the teaching on the value of the law and the prophets and Christ's own example of breaking the sabbath?

3. Should christians today offer the other cheek or walk two miles with a man who forces them to go one? Which one of us would give a coat to a beggar whom we saw in a city street in winter time?

Mt 6:1–18. Good deeds in secret—the Lord's prayer

Now Matthew turns to the question of how good deeds should be done. Again he gives first the general principle and then the application to the three classic good works of judaism: almsgiving, prayer and fasting. In each of these he uses the same set of formulae: 'When you . . . do not act as the hypocrites. I tell you solemnly, they have had their reward. But when you . . . in secret, and your Father who sees all that is done in secret will reward you.' The lesson, then, is a general one which concerns all good actions, though Matthew makes the application only to three classic examples. Its importance is shown by its recurrence else-where in the gospels, for example in Matthew's condemna-tion of ostentation by the Pharisees, and Luke's parable of the Pharisee and the publican at prayer.

Into this plea for simplicity and purity the evangelist inserts the Lord's prayer. As in the case of the beatitudes, Matthew slightly expands Luke's more primitive version (Luke, for instance, has just 'Father', and no 'your will be done' phrase); Matthew's version gains in fullness but loses in directness and simplicity. To the disciples the striking element above all others was the familiarity of calling God simply 'Father'—so striking that Matthew adds 'in heaven' to avoid confusion. The way Jesus ad-dressed God as his father, and told his disciples to do the same, set the tone, in Paul's eyes, for the whole relation-ship of the christian to God. The Spirit which constitutes a man a christian is the Spirit 'in which we cry "Abba, Father"'. Here Paul retains the Aramaic word which must have stood at the head of the Lord's prayer. It means not merely 'father' but the familiar 'daddy' used by children to their father. This nearness to God was so unbelievable that the early christians, though not understanding Aramaic, held on to this one word 'Abba' as a guarantee of the relationship. It was even more striking against the background of the contemporary Jewish attitude to God, which stressed only his kingship, majesty and infinite transcendence, so that his love as a father was quite forgotten under the fear and awe which were the predominant notes in their relationship to him. Beginning as it does with this call to the Father, the Lord's prayer is then primarily a prayer of children that all their father's purposes may come about, and at the same time a pledge of cooperation in this.

The first three petitions are substantially the same, centred on 'your kingdom come'. By the coming of the kingdom God's name is made holy, since his power and his love of his people (these are the connotations of his 'name', his dominant characteristics) are recognised by all who see his action in establishing the kingdom for his people. And this is the accomplishment of his will, since he wills above all that his kingdom should be achieved and completed; in the old testament indeed the accomplishment of God's will has, besides its obvious sense, the special connotation of the fulfilment of his plan of salvation and the re-establishment of perfect harmony between man and God.

The second of the two stanzas concerns man's immediate needs. Matthew places particular emphasis on forgiveness, since he adds a saying of Jesus on this subject immediately after the prayer. Forgiveness plays a major part in his concept of relations between christian brothers, for it dominates chapter 18, the collection of sayings about fraternal relations, culminating in the command to forgive seventy times seven times, and the threatening parable of the unmerciful servant. If we take the last two petitions together there seems to be an allusion to the great testing time of the final crisis, in which the evil one will make his last efforts to prevent the final establishment of the kingdom. Although it is a privilege from God to undergo the purification given by such an ordeal, we need not pretend that we are undergoing ordeals; this prayer shows that it is legitimate to follow Jesus' example at the agony when he prayed that this cup might pass from him.

1. For modern times, so keen on finding authenticity in the man–God relation, how can we find a place for prayer in church, in the community of God's people? Is one not always hypocritical in church, praying in public?

2. Do we have faith enough to pray to God in the intimate way which Jesus allowed us? Where in modern life can we find the real knowledge that Jesus' Father cares for us as a human father?

3. Isn't it cowardly and distrustful to ask to be spared temptation?

Mt 6:19–34. On single-mindedness

Matthew continues the lesson of the earlier part of the chapter with a collection of sayings whose central theme is filial trust in God and utter generosity, in expectation of reward from him alone. This is the expression in action of real confidence in his power and his fatherly love; this is shown to be the sense of the passage because Matthew inserts 'your heavenly Father' where his source (as shown by Luke) has only 'God'. The usual translations would suggest that all the christian's worry should be about the kingdom; but the Greek word denotes not merely care (let alone worry) but toil over ordinary household tasks. It means, then, that all our energy in daily life, not merely our worries, should be devoted to the kingdom. But in assessing how literally this counsel should be taken— should one positively neglect ordinary household and family cares and tasks?—it must be remembered that Jesus commonly uses an energetic, over-contrasting, semitic way of speaking which can seem too black-and-white to us. When Jesus says 'If any man comes to me without hating his father, mother, etc . . . he cannot be my disciple' (Lk 14:26) he is hardly speaking literally according to modern use of terms: we would probably use a comparative form 'If a man does not put me before father, mother, etc . . .'

> *1. Does this interpretation water down Jesus' message?*
> *2. Modern man is worried about money more than anything else. On this depends his social status, his importance in the world, his self-respect, etc. Jesus contrasts the kingdom and money. Do we in fact put this into our practice of christianity?*

Mt 7:1–29. Conclusion of the sermon on the mount

These sayings seem at first sight to form a heterogeneous cluster, merely thrown together at the end of the discourse. But the chapter has in fact a coherent pattern. The instructional part of the sermon ends at 7:12 with a summary which is true to the whole tone of the ethic of active fraternal love in this gospel: 'always treat others as you would like them to treat you.' This is the completion of the teaching of the old law which was proclaimed at the beginning of the sermon.

Before this Matthew sets a final warning against judging and a final exhortation to prayer, each driven home with a set of images. In each of these the name of God is reverently avoided, so that what is really meant is:

Do not judge and God will not judge you.
Ask, and God will give . . . knock and God will open
the door to you.

But the images speak for themselves.

After the conclusion in 7:12 comes a series of parables
in contrasts, such as Matthew particularly loves:

The narrow gate and the broad road.
The sound tree with good fruit and the rotten tree with
bad fruit.
The man who just says 'Lord, Lord' and the man who
acts.
The man who builds on rock and the man who builds
on sand.

Most of these are traditional images used in the old testament. It is interesting that the metaphor of a house built
on rock is used of the solidity enjoyed by those who obey
the law; its application here suggests that the teaching
just given is Jesus' new law which has now superseded the
old. Perhaps the most striking is the third, which seems
to be without parallel in Jewish literature; it comes again
in a slightly fuller form in 21:28–32, and one can well
picture Jesus originally using this parable against self-
righteous Pharisees who claimed to do what was right in
God's eyes but did not act out the claim.

*1. Jesus insists that we must act, not merely pay lip
service to the gospel. What do we actually do to show both
our love of God and our love of mankind? What is our
attitude to those who are spiritually and materially poor
in the world?*

*2. Do we have to be perfect before we can criticise
others?*

4

Ten miracles
Mt 8:1–9:35

The narrative section which opens the second of the five books of Matthew's gospel is devoted to miracles. The evangelist, with his usual systematisation, gathers ten miracles from various places, mostly in Mark (though he also leaves the last two in their original places, so that they occur twice in his gospel), to form a single group broken only by two short interludes. Systematisation is not however the sole purpose, for by this means he also gives a forceful impression of Jesus' miraculous activity. The general lesson, taught by these miracles with many different nuances, is that he is the messiah, restoring all things, removing the evil of disease, curbing the forces of evil seen in diabolical possession, and restoring the forces of nature to their due subjection to the harmony with man. This fulfilled the expectation that the messiah would bring a renewal which would also be a return to the original state of peace and happiness. It would be absurd to pretend that since his coming there have been no more suffering, evil and discord: we believe that he has fundamentally restored peace and that through this action of his suffering, evil and discord will disappear. His miracles are physical and visible signs of this, pledges, so to speak, of the task he is to complete.

Mt 8:1–17. Four miraculous cures

Each of these cures has its own special point, but common to them all is the demand for faith so clearly expressed in the first. In his editing of Mark's miracle-stories Matthew often leaves out many of the lively and engaging details which show Mark to be such a superb storyteller, and files the story down till only the skeleton remains. But this skeleton always shows that those who are granted the miracle have faith in Jesus; since the miracles are signs, unless there is an openness to see their significance, Jesus does not grant them (as at Nazareth, 13:58). The skeleton also retains, and indeed highlights, elements which show Jesus' dignity: the reverence paid him, his natural authority and power of command. The very reticence and brevity of the narratives lends Jesus a statuesque quality which is certainly not unintentional; any mention in Mark of emotion on Jesus' part is rigidly excluded. The result is an impression of the Lord akin to that given by the great solemn Christ of a Byzantine mosaic.

The cure of leprosy has a special quality because it was considered both a special affliction sent by God (so that to cure it shows that Jesus was, if not God, at least very closely linked to him) and 'a living death', since it cut a man off from everything which made life worth living. 'Leprosy' is used in the Greek of the period for many different, often quite mild, skin diseases; but those suffering from the more virulent forms were expelled from society and lived as vagrant outcasts.

The cure of the centurion's servant is remarkable for the recognition accorded to Jesus by a gentile, and the solemn promise with which Jesus responds (a saying of Jesus not found at this point in Luke's version of the

incident, but inserted from elsewhere). As in the case of
the contrast between Herod's venom against and the wise
men's reverence for the child Jesus, Matthew underlines
how the Jews, the 'children of the kingdom', forfeit their
privileges by unbelief, while the gentiles show the faith
the Jews lack.

The cure of Simon Peter's mother-in-law is obviously
a family story of the apostles. In Mark there is the turmoil
of a peasant's crowded croft, but in Matthew the atmosphere is one of sacred stillness in the presence of Christ.

Finally we have a summary of Jesus' curing work, and
Matthew points out how this too fulfils the prophecies.

*1. Faith in God is unpopular at the present day, when
we are both learning more about the world and finding
the way to dominate our environment more and more.
Does this alter our attitude to miracles?*

*2. Were Jesus' cures faith-healing? Would it matter if
they were?*

*3. 'The subjects of the kingdom will be turned out
into the dark'. Does this apply to all the Jews? Has it
already occurred? To whom else might it apply, and why?*

Mt 8:18–22. The call to follow Christ

A brief interlude in which Jesus shows the absolute and
total demands of discipleship. In the second saying there
is implied a contrast with the call of Elisha (1 Kgs 19: 19–
21); this was less demanding, for he was allowed first to
say good-bye to his family.

How are we to express our trust in God today?

Mt 8:23–27. The calming of a storm

Nature-miracles such as this one resist all attempts at
natural explanations by hypnosis or the faith of the sub-

ject. But we are learning more and more that exceptional people sometimes have exceptional power over beasts and the lower creation, though never to anything approaching the degree here shown. It would be a perfectly reasonable explanation that Jesus, who was without parallel exceptional, should have such powers over nature, as a unique extension of the little manipulations of nature which are reported as observed facts. In Jewish eyes this control of the sea has special importance, because traditionally it was God alone who controlled the storm and the potentially evil monster which was the deep; hence the awe and astonishment of the disciples. Against the background such an act of control of nature —even if not without weak analogies in nature-control by other men—is a most forceful demonstration of what God's power would do when incarnate in a man.

Mt 8:28–34. The demoniacs of Gadara

The pigs in this story are so picturesque and so pathetic that they have captured the popular imagination, and from being a mere accessory to show the destructive force of the spirits cast out by Jesus, they have come to overshadow the real point of the story. There are of course real problems about them: no one has yet succeeded in finding a plausible locale for the miracle, since Gadara is some ten miles from the Lake of Galilee, and Gerasa (the name given by Mark) is thirty; either of these makes a long run for a pig. Further, by what right does Jesus destroy them? Some claim that it was because Jews were forbidden to keep pigs, an unclean animal; but it is unlikely that the owner was a Jew, since the incident occurs in a non-Jewish area, and unproven that pig-keeping was forbidden at this era.

More important is the whole question of diabolical

possession. How are we to interpret this? It is certainly reported still to occur in 'primitive' countries, and we must not shirk the truth that the evangelists, and Jesus himself, were men of their time and culture, inevitably thinking in the terms then current. The real difficulty of the pigs is this: mental illness can be cured by hypnosis, and Jesus in virtue of his divine and messianic power certainly had a power of command over the minds of men. But that a mental illness should be transferred from one sufferer to another (especially from a man to a pig) fits the primitive image of diabolical spirits but not the medical realities. A possible solution is that at some point in the transmission of the story the element of the pigs was added, though not part of the original miracle, as a tangible demonstration of the force of the illness.

Possession can clearly find an analogy among people suffering from mental disease. But what about those who are sinful? What does sin do to a man? Does it make him unsociable? Does it mean that he in some sense loses control of himself and can hardly stop himself behaving in a way that can only harm himself and others. What about the sacrament of confession? Is that a parallel with Jesus evicting what are called evil spirits in the gospel?

Mt 9:1–8. Cure of a sick man

In this story the cure of the illness is quite incidental, for the sickness may have been very minor; 'paralytic' means no more than 'confined to bed'. The main point is the challenge to the scribes. Jesus seems to provoke them deliberately, for the sick man's friends merely wanted his illness to be cured, but Jesus provokes the scribes by squarely claiming a power not associated with the messiah but belonging to God alone, that of forgiving sins.

In this way he shows what it means when a man is God. All the way through the story there are hints that, though the scribes think that they are evaluating Jesus, in fact he is in a position to judge them.

But is the conclusion satisfactory? We are left with a sense that the scribes were too easily convinced, for the physical cure can hardly be taken as evidence of the forgiveness of sins, which demands divine power. Perhaps Jesus is playing on the popular belief that disease is the result of sin, not merely of the imperfection of the world in general, but of the sin of the individual who suffers the illness; so when he is cured it is a sign that his sin has been forgiven.

There is a little hint at the end of Matthew's account, where he departs from Mark, who is his source for the rest of the story. 'They praised God for giving such power to men' is not strictly fair, since only one man has been seen to have the power. But clearly Matthew is thinking of the church's power to give God's forgiveness, connecting it in this way with Jesus' action.

1. Why do the scribes take up this attitude against Jesus? What is our attitude when we are shown to be wrong in our ideas and ways of thinking? Do we 'do down' our opponents, be it in matters of religion, politics, war?

2. Is there any connection between sin and sickness? What is it?

Mt 9:9–13. The call of Matthew

There are two puzzling factors about the call of this apostle: firstly Mark and Luke in their versions of the story give him the name of Levi, a name which does not appear in any of the versions of lists of the twelve.

Secondly it is tolerably clear from the rest of the gospel
that its writer was not familiar with details of Palestinian
geography, as he must have been had he lived in Capernaum and followed Jesus. He would also have been a
very old man when he wrote the gospel (which probably
stems from after 80 AD in its final form), if he had been
one of Jesus' group of followers. Furthermore it is
obvious that he draws his information not from his own
memory of Jesus' actions but from two sources, the gospel
of Mark and a collection of the sayings of Jesus; these
in their turn depended only indirectly on eye-witness
accounts, and were directly derived from the traditions
of Jesus' life preserved in the christian communities of
the Mediterranean world. What, then, are we to make of
the substitution in our gospel of the name Matthew for
the name Levi which occurs in the others? Perhaps the
author changed the name from Levi because this name
does not appear in the lists of the apostles, and chose
Matthew as a substitute because it was under Matthew's
patronage that the gospel was published.

Also in the story which follows Matthew makes an
interesting change of emphasis. Mark's version is centred
on Jesus' person, on the welcome he extends to all sinners
who turn to him. But Matthew, by inserting the verse
'What I want is mercy, not sacrifice,' changes this to a
direct attack on the observance of the Jewish ritual law.
It is not the ritual law as such which he attacks (indeed he
sometimes shows that he retains some attachment to it),
but the observance of it in priority or even in opposition
to the claims of love; he attacks the rigidity which puts
legal correctness first and humanity second.

   *1. Can one's attitude to church law be the same as
Matthew's to the Jewish law, disobeying it whenever*

obedience to it would not be an expression of love for
God and other people?

2. *Do catholics in particular tend to be superstitious*
about observance of church law?

3. *What is our attitude not only to sinners such as*
prostitutes and thieves, murderers, the more glamour-
ously sinful, but this worse type of sinner—the proud,
the self-sufficient, the modern Pharisee? Should we try to
love such people too? If so, how?

Mt 9 : 14–17. A discussion on fasting

Here gathered together are three vivid images to show
how radical is the break between christianity and judaism; christianity cannot be simply sewn onto or poured
into the old forms. But yet the first of these shows that
there can be at least a degree of external similarity between them, for fasting is permitted in each, though for
different motives. Is it stretching the text to see in 9 : 15
a hint that the christian motive for fasting is union with
Christ in his passion? All three images of a marriage
feast, a new garment and new wine hark back to images
used in the prophecies that the messiah will bring about
a totally new world of happiness and plenty; this was
primarily what Jesus was teaching, and it is only through
their present position that they reinforce the teaching of
the previous passage about the relationship of christianity
to judaism.

Are such ascetical practices as fasting still profitable?

Mt 9 : 18–35. Four miraculous cures and a summary

To conclude his group of ten miracles Matthew now
gives us four cures. The first two are taken from Mark

with again additional emphasis on two aspects: the noble dignity of Jesus (much less of the jostling, noisy crowds), and the faith and reverence of those who ask the miracle. The same elements appear also in the last two miracles, but these are not taken from Mark; the former appears to be a slightly altered version of the cure of the blind men at Jericho in 20:29–34, and the latter (which is rather vague and general, without any concrete detail) seems to have been made up by Matthew. These literary processes seem rather dubious to a modern reader; but it appears that conventions were different in the first century. The evangelist knew that Jesus worked all kinds of miracles and, to make up his number of ten, felt justified in composing two little stories.

Is Matthew here being dishonest?

5

Instructions for apostles
Mt 10:1–42

Matthew gives his collection of sayings of Jesus about the apostolate an introduction consisting of two sayings on the motive for such activity and a list of Jesus' own chosen band of twelve apostles. There are four versions of this list in the new testament, each with one or two minor changes among the less well-known names; it seems that what was clearly remembered—and so what was most important—was not the identity of the individuals but the number twelve, perhaps because they corresponded to the founders of the twelve tribes of the old Israel. Is this because their authority was exercised not by the individual members but as a college, as indeed is evident in Acts? They were far more than apostles or missioners, but were the solid foundations on which was built the whole christian community; this is why they receive such a special formation about Jesus' person and message in the section of the gospel which begins after this collection of sayings about the apostolate.

The motive given for apostolic work is primarily love and care for the 'sheep without a shepherd' who are exploited and oppressed, presumably by their present religious leaders, though these are no more than the embodiment at the time of the forces of error and especially of timorous narrowness. This is one of the few echoes in the other gospels of John's parable of the good shepherd. To this is added the saying about the harvest; this might suggest that the work of harvesting is for the benefit not of those harvested but of the owner of the harvest (?God). In reality it is a figure intended to convey the pressing need for haste; once the crops are ready they cannot remain standing for long; so, once the messiah has come, his followers must do all they can to hasten the full coming of his kingdom.

1. In what sense are the bishops the embodiment to us of the apostles, and in what sense not?

2. Is it really a duty to spread the faith? Have 'men of good will' anything further to gain from it than they already possess?

Mt 10:5–16. How an apostle acts

Here is a collection of varied instructions given, no doubt on different occasions, by Jesus, to those who were to spread his message. They are not complete or systematic, but one can discern certain central emphases. One of the most striking is the total simplicity of the messenger of Christ, travelling with no reserves but relying at each moment on God's care as shown in the generosity of men. But Jesus is not so naive as to suppose that the good will needed is to be found everywhere. It is, however, only the barest minimum of good will that is demanded under serious threat, for to break the laws of hospitality is still a heinous crime in the Near East. But Jesus recognises that even so it will be denied.

1. Can one usually detect some lack of goodwill in those who reject Christ's message?

2. Who are 'apostles' today? To what extent does their picture still correspond to these instructions?

Mt 10:17–25. How an apostle suffers

The lot of an apostle is persecution, by both religious and civil authorities, the sanhedrin and the governors and kings respectively. The sermon on the mount has already said that the blessedness of all christians, not only apostles (but is it possible to be a christian without being an apostle?), lies in this. Here the application of this saying is made especially to apostles, and it is added that this persecution is not only for Christ's sake but after the model of Christ himself. In the upheaval within the church in recent years it has so often been those who have borne persecution patiently who have turned out to be the real prophets and apostles who have deepened the church's understanding of herself and of theology.

Matthew also gives briefly a saying which is the centre of an important theme in John, that the Spirit of the Father—or, as John says, Christ's own Spirit—will be speaking in the apostles. This is tantamount to saying that Christ himself will be present and speaking through them, since the Spirit which he sends is to grant Christ's own real presence and power in the church.

1. Have we ever experienced this ability to say the right thing when put in a tight spot by those who would like in some way to harm us or criticise us when we have been working for good and truth? If not, why not? Because of lack of faith?

2. How can we tell when and in whom Christ is speaking in the church?

Mt 10:26–42. The challenge and the reward of following Christ

Matthew concludes this collection of sayings about the apostolate of the followers of Christ with a varied group

of sayings, some of which occur in other parts of the
gospel in slightly different form, as though they had been
handed down through different channels of the oral
tradition (e.g. 10:34–36 are very similar to 10:21;
10:38–39 to 16:24–25). There is no single theme, but
many points are touched upon: the absolute demands of
putting Christ first in all things, the command to spread
his message to the world, the opposition which Christ's
messenger must expect and the confidence he may have
in facing it, the reward which those who carry on Christ's
work will have, as being themselves other Christs, if only
they surrender their all to his service.

*1. If christianity is of the truth, then why are so many
christians afraid that their position and codes of behaviour are threatened?*

*2. Can our concern for the true good of others force us
christians to impose certain disciplines and codes of behaviour on others?*

*3. Which of us is so convinced of the value of follow-
ing Christ that he will quarrel with his own close relatives?*

6
The great division
Mt 11:1–12:50

After the sayings on the apostolate comes the next narrative section of the gospel, leading up to the revelation of the nature of the kingdom in parables (13:1–52). Parables are fully understood only by Christ's own disciples, so that it is hardly surprising that they should be placed after a section where there is considerable development in the division between those who accept and follow Christ, and those who reject him. This seems to be the common theme which binds all the passages of chapters 11 and 12 together; the world is divided into two camps, for and against Jesus.

Mt 11:1–15. The question of John the Baptist
The opposition to Jesus underlies and gives the tone to this passage from the beginning, since the Baptist has been imprisoned; his arrest and execution stand in the long series of rejections of prophets by the Jews which will culminate in the arrest and execution of Jesus. But towards the end of the incident Jesus shows that this rejection of God's messengers has entered a new phase and reached a new intensity since John, who stands on the very threshold of the kingdom. Lawless violence is now directed not merely against the heralds of the kingdom but against the kingdom itself, and such men are

attempting to push away the kingdom (the opposite of 'thy kingdom come') and prevent others entering it.

One of the chief interests of the passage is that it shows the real divergence between the Baptist and Jesus. Jesus is full of praise for the Baptist; he is a prophet, and not merely a prophet but the figure promised under various images in the old testament who was to precede the final coming by God, the great visitation which would inaugurate the new world; this is what Jesus meant by identifying him with Elijah and with the messenger who would prepare the way before God. But the interesting thing is that the Baptist does not seem to have seen himself in this role; he denied that he was Elijah (Jn 1:21, 25), and regarded himself as the herald of the eschatological figure who was to prepare the way for God's coming, whom he saw to be Jesus. The Baptist seems to have envisaged one stage more than did Jesus: herald— eschatological figure—final visitation, whereas Jesus envisaged only herald—eschatological figure whose coming is the final visitation and inauguration of the new world. But had we not the realisation of it in Jesus, the Baptist's interpretation of the complex and manifold Jewish messianic hope would have seemed legitimate enough. There were so many variations in their hopes that a good deal of divergence in interpretation was unavoidable.

There was another point in which Jesus did not correspond to the Baptist's expectations, and it was this which led to his question. It is clear from his preaching that the figure the Baptist was expecting was one of fire, judgement and retribution. Though he had pointed out Jesus as the one who was to come, when Jesus did not fulfil this programme, John seems to have had doubts, and hence sent to ask if he were really the one who was to come. Jesus' reply is that he is indeed this figure, but that John has misunderstood the meaning of this figure, who is a figure of mercy and healing, restoring rather than destroying, giving life rather than dealing death. All this he indicates by describing his activity in terms which would inevitably recall those of Isaiah in which he describes the restoration and renewal prophesied for the last time; it is the Hebrew way of saying: '*This* is what I fulfil', and this, rather than the actual healing which they bestowed, is the primary meaning of the miracles.

1. What can we learn about our own doubts of faith from the doubts of John the Baptist?

2. What does it mean: 'Men of violence take the Kingdom of God by force'? How much violence, and of what kind, should there be in our actions for gaining the kingdom of God?

Mt 11:16–30. Lament over the stubborn, invitation to the simple

The contrast continues; Jesus points out the cussedness, like the uncooperative sulks of children, of Jews who find fault both with John's asceticism and equally with his own breadth of spirit. It is now not merely that they are shocked by his actions in disregarding propriety by eating with outcasts; now they are prepared to find fault whatever he does. The lament over the cities which follows seems to stem from a late stage in Jesus' ministry in Galilee, when these towns have totally failed to respond; Luke places it on the final journey to Jerusalem. Matthew, however, anticipates in order to stress the division which is already happening. It is noticeable that Jesus does not himself condemn these cities or any who refuse his message; their condemnation comes from themselves, and Jesus is merely prohesying, not prescribing, their destruction (the black and desolate ruins of Chorazin especially are an impressive confirmation of the prophecy). The biblical forms 'Alas for . . .' and 'Blessed he who . . .' are not prayers for the accomplishment of a curse or a blessing, but statements of fact.

The reference to Tyre and Sidon, whose haughtiness was a byword in the old testament, and the quotation from Isaiah, suggest that it is the pride of the lakeside towns that Jesus especially singles out. In absolute contrast is the thanksgiving hymn which follows. A feature of this, which is the more striking because totally new in Jewish thinking, is the favoured position of the underprivileged and unlearned. The law had become so all-important in Jewish life that a sort of aristocracy of scholars of the law had developed, and an enormous premium was put upon study of the law as the passport to respectability and sanctity; in many cases this was allied to a certain harshness and snobbishness characteristic of learned societies. Against this Jesus presents an absolute paradox: he identifies himself with three central figures of the old dispensation, three privileged sources of knowledge of God, and proclaims that it is in himself alone, not in acquired learning, that the most despised, oppressed and unlearned find the knowledge. These three self-identifications of Jesus are valuable to us, though obviously couched in extremely Jewish concepts, as showing Jesus' own awareness of himself and of his relationship to the Father. Firstly he indicates that he incarnates the old testament figure of wisdom. In the last centuries before Christ a doctrine of divine wisdom working in the world had developed, which saw in a personification of wisdom the expression of the power by which God created and orders the world. Jesus now claims to be this wisdom, by claiming several of its attributes.

Only God fully knows his wisdom, and only his wisdom fully knows God—so with Jesus here; in wisdom alone will man find rest—so also in Jesus. Secondly, Jesus claims to be the fulfilment of the mysterious figure of Daniel's prophetic vision, when he saw a Son of Man coming to God in heaven and receiving from God all power and sovereignty over the world and all nations; this Jesus receives as man, a stupendous claim for a Galilean peasant, founded on his relationship to the Father. Thirdly, Jesus claims to be the new law, in telling men to take on themselves no longer the yoke of the law (an unmistakably familiar phrase to the Jews) but his own yoke, which contrasts with that of the law, in that it brings rest and relief instead of a heavy burden. Jesus, a Jew reared in the Jewish tradition, naturally expressed his consciousness of his personality and his role in terms which rely on the scriptures.

1. Jesus says that his yoke is easy and his burden light. Do we really find this to be so?

2. Is prayer 'foolish'? Are good works 'foolish'? What of loving others? What of loving God, unseen and unfelt yet known to be there?

Mt 12:1–8. Picking corn on the sabbath

At first it may seem that the lesson of this story is that the sabbath has no binding force any longer: this is indeed the lesson in Mark's version. But Matthew poses a trickier problem. It appears from a number of little alterations which he makes to the text he received from Mark that in his community the sabbath was still observed. Though he retains Mark's statement that the Son of Man is Lord of the sabbath, his main problem is on what principles such a law as sabbath observance may be broken. He is

careful to insist that the disciples did not break it casually
(as in Mark) but only because of real need, just as in the
scriptural parallel which justifies their conduct. He then
advances to the general principle about the observance
of law: 'What I want is love not sacrifice'; it is for neglect-
ing this that the Pharisees will be condemned, for love is
the criterion of all conduct in Matthew. The word used
for 'love' or 'mercy' conjures up a whole world of old
testament allusion, for it is the word which stands for
God's constant care, his tender guidance of Israel, his
burning and watchful love of his people, ever forgiving
and calling back. This is the quality which is demanded
of men, and which Matthew puts here as superior to law.

What is the point of outward observance of religious
and moral law? Could a man who refused to conform in
any outward way to the twentieth-century norms of christ-
ian behaviour be called a follower of Christ?

Mt 12:9–21. Cure of the man with a withered hand

Another story of the mounting opposition between Jesus
and the leaders of the Jews, which ends in their decision
to do away with him, seemingly without any spark of
goodwill or understanding towards him. In Matthew's
version this is the worse because Matthew has inserted
an isolated saying of Jesus (given in another context by
Luke) which gives a perfectly good rabbinic argument
to justify his action on a sabbath, using as starting point
the rabbinic ruling that it was permissible thus to extract
an animal from a hole on the sabbath. The principle
is again that formal ritual law yields to the dictates of
love and human sympathy. But this does not mollify his
opponents.

After this incident Matthew adds a scriptural quota-

tion to show how the spirit of Jesus' conduct fulfils the
hopes for the messiah expressed by Isaiah. He is the
servant of the Lord, healing and restoring, and so showing the nature of the Spirit of the Lord.

*1. How important are ritual observances and exacti-
tude in fulfilling them?*

*2. How important is observance of Sunday? What
forms should it take? How does it relate to the sabbath?*

Mt 12:22–37. The Spirit of God and Beelzebul

In this passage we can well see the formation of the
gospel tradition taking place. According to Mark (who
has nothing corresponding to Mt 12:27–28, 30 and 32a)
to the Jews' accusations Jesus just throws down some
challenging images, whose application they must work
out for themselves; this corresponds to 12:25–26 and 29
in Matthew. Then follows a threat 'because they were
saying "An unclean spirit is in him"' (Mk 3:30)
against those who speak sacrilegiously against the Holy
Spirit (or the Spirit of God). For Matthew this is not
clear enough, so he combines Mark's account with some
other sayings of Jesus.

In any case the advent of the messiah is firmly linked
in Jewish thought with the end of Satan's or Beelzebul's
tyranny. So the audience were to conclude from the challenge of the sayings in Mark (taken over into Mt 12:25–
26 and 29) that the reign of the messiah had suddenly
arrived; this conclusion is drawn by the saying in
Mt 12:27–28. But the addition in Mt 12:32a instead of clarifying makes things more obscure: how can
one say a word against the Son of Man without saying
a word also against the Holy Spirit in whose power he
works, as the whole passage has been showing? Perhaps

the solution is that the saying belongs to another context, in which it is envisaged that someone might fail to recognise that Jesus, the Son of Man, was acting in the power of the Holy Spirit. This would certainly fit the context which the saying is given by Luke (12:10).

1. How can we now try to gain a vision of what our lives should be about, and not allow ourselves to be as blind as so many of those who saw and heard Jesus himself were?

2. How seriously should one take 12:37? Does it refer simply to words, or deeds too?

Mt 12:38–45. The sign of Jonah

The theme here is the contrast between the Jews and other nations. In the tale of Jonah the men of Nineveh responded immediately to God's messenger; the non-Jewish Queen of the South (popularly the Queen of Sheba) recognised the wisdom of God in Solomon; but the Jews do not acknowledge the messenger of God and the wisdom of God in Jesus. Again we are confronted with the mystery of how God's people, so carefully prepared and kept faithful for centuries, failed when the testing time came.

The great sign given by Jesus was the sign of the resurrection, to which all other signs led up (Matthew carefully says, however, that this generation 'asks for a sign *in addition*'). This is God's guarantee of Jesus as his messenger, as the liberation of Jonah from the belly of the sea-beast was his guarantee of Jonah. Matthew adds two references to the time of three days and three nights. These are not in the more primitive version given by Luke, and do not fit Jesus' case exactly (Friday afternoon to Sunday morning). The further question may also be asked here for the first time: how far did Jesus know what were to be the exact details of his passion?

Mt 12:46–50. True brethren of Jesus

During this whole section of the gospel from the beginning of chapter 11 the gap has been becoming clearer between the Jews as a whole and those who accept Jesus. Now it concludes with a little scene which shows that mere blood-relationship with Jesus is not enough to make a man one of his brethren in the christian sense of the word. Jesus' brothers (the Aramaic word is as loose as our 'cousins') stand for the people as a whole, and are contrasted with the crowds who had followed him and so done the will of the Father. But why his mother too? This is unambiguously Mary, and hence the scene, though it does not show disrespect for her, does not show the respect and warmth towards her which we would expect. It does seem, also from the marriage feast at Cana, that Jesus showed a certain distance towards his mother during the public ministry. Perhaps this was as an example that a man must be prepared to abandon all ties to follow him, even those of the family.

1. With our present understanding of the old testament we would never use the Jonah story in the way Jesus does. Is this a difficulty for us?

2. The development of catholic theology has made of Mary something very different from the figure we glimpse from time to time in passages such as this. Does it matter?

7

Parables
Mt 13:1–52

Two great problems overshadow the gospel parables: how close are they to the parables pronounced by Jesus? Why did he teach in parables? To the second question the answer would seem to be obvious: storytelling is an unrivalled method of teaching a lesson, not only to primitive people and children (Adam and Eve, the book of Jonah, *The Water Babies*) but also to the more sophisticated (*Animal Farm*, *The Lord of the Flies*); Jesus naturally resorted to this way, well known in judaism, of teaching the nature of the kingdom he had come to found. He had a difficult lesson to get across, for most people expected the kingdom to be a political one, established in fire and fury; he had to show that the spirit of his kingdom was quite different, that it was a kingdom which included sinners, that, though it was to change the world, it started from small and unimpressive beginnings. For these lessons the ideal vehicle was the series of word-images which Jesus gave. Yet the evangelists do not say that Jesus' purpose was to help the people to understand. Mark, on the contrary, indicates that he used parables 'so that they may hear, and hear again, but not understand' (4:12); for him parables are a deliberate veiling. For Matthew teaching in parables is the result of the lack of comprehension of the crowds, a sort of penalty

(13:13), which is at any rate less shocking than Mark's deliberate mystification.

It has been suggested that this theory of the parables is a subsequent one, invented to explain why Jesus was not widely acclaimed: because he deliberately made his message unintelligible to all but an inner circle of disciples. Another theory is that the word translated 'parables' in 13:13 should really mean 'riddles' (the same Aramaic word underlies both), and that Jesus really meant 'the fact that they find my teaching riddles and unintelligible fulfils the prophet Isaiah', without any special reference to what we now know as the parables.

The problem becomes easier if it is considered alongside the first of our two questions; for the parables were surely more obscure to the writers of the gospels than to their first hearers. There were two reasons for this: firstly, the parables were handed down as stories without the context in which they were first told, so that their precise point was often hard to re-establish, without knowledge of the situation which gave them their relevance in Jesus' life. The evangelists assumed that their relevance must be primarily to their own church-situation; in fact it was primarily to Jesus' situation and only secondarily to that of the church. Secondly, the few full explanations of parables which we have (eg Mt 13:20-23, 36-43) suggest that Matthew at any rate understood the parables as allegories, in which there was a one-to-one equivalent in the interpretation for every element in the story; these interpretations betray the language and interests of the early church rather than those of Jesus.

Does this mean that the evangelists got the parables wrong? No, only that they applied them so eagerly to their own missionary situation and vivid expectation of the approaching end of the world that they give us little help towards seeing how Jesus intended his own hearers to understand them. This is no easy task.

Mt 13:1-9. Parable of the sower and (13:18-23) its interpretation

It seems indubitable that the framework in which the evangelists set this parable, as most other single incidents in the gospels, is artificial; to understand its message we must attempt to reconstruct its original setting. Jesus must have reflected on the failure of his mission to the people as a whole, which has already shown itself in the gospel. Most refused his message, some were perhaps attracted for a time; only a few accepted whole-heartedly, but in these his joy was great. Such could be the background, in Jesus' own reflection, to the image of the sower; this is even more attractive in Mark's optimistic version, which ends with an upward twist: thirtyfold, sixtyfold, a hundredfold, instead of Matthew's decreasing hundred, sixty, thirty.

In the interpretation of the parable the missionary atmosphere of the early church is apparent: persecution and the lure of riches are alike out of place in Jesus' own little group; many of the terms, 'the word' for the news of Christ, a 'root' standing for stability, and others, are technical terms of the early church unknown in Christ's own ministry. But the application of Jesus' reflection on his own partial success, limited in extent but encouraging in depth, to the situation of the apostolic preaching is in strict continuity; the same holds true of each. Only the simple folk by the lake could never have been expected to understand all this about a situation of which they could have had no experience. But in addition the emphasis has changed: instead of being a reflection on Jesus' situation, in which joy is tempered by disappointment, the parable serves as a warning to christians not to be distracted from their fidelity.

1. According to the gospel, belonging to Christ and belonging to this world are contradictory. Yet the second Vatican council and all modern christianity tell us to be more involved in this world. How then can we reconcile these views? How can one avoid being stifled by the world's cares?

2. In this life is there more value in prayer or in works? Be honest!

Mt 13:24–43. The tares, the mustard-seed and the leaven

What was the central point of these parables in Jesus' mouth? We know that the disciples were often impatient, wanting the kingdom to be made manifest, with themselves in places of honour. Did the parable of the tares teach them that they must wait a while? Did the mustard-seed and the leaven teach that their insignificant little group had yet a great task to perform?

Matthew's interpretation of the parable of the tares looks at it, characteristically, from the point of view of our chances on the day of judgement—a constant preoccupation of his. His concentration on this one point—and it is his, for both theology and language of these verses are unmistakably matthean—is only one-sided, not illegitimate. It is not Jesus' point of view, but it is an inference from the parable. We shall often find that the Jewish picture of the day of judgement serves as a backcloth and point of reference in his theology.

1. One of the most difficult tasks of man is to live among people who are insufficient and incapable; this is

*all the more painful for those who try to live by the light
of the gospel, and who can in all humility see how other
so called christians abuse the gospel. What should be our
attitude in these circumstances?*

*2. How do we feel if we are unnoticed in our work as
christians? Should we seek the limelight to proclaim the
gospel?*

Mt 13:44–52. The treasure, the pearl and the dragnet

The collection of seven parables about the kingdom
closes with three brief images. The first two form a pair,
but is their lesson the joy which those who find the kingdom should have in it, or that the kingdom is hidden
and needs a persevering search? The dragnet is very
similar to the tares, and similarly receives a little matthean 'key' to the allegory at the end.

8
The training of the disciples
Mt 13:53–17:27

Jesus now begins to concentrate on training the disciples who will carry on his work, no longer seeking to spread his message directly among the people as a whole or their leaders. The scenes in this part of the gospel (13:53–17:27) concentrate always on the disciples. But first come two stories to confirm Jesus' rejection by the people as a whole: his rejection by his own townsfolk at Nazareth, and Herod's rejection of Jesus' forerunner and herald.

Mt 13:53–58. Rejection at Nazareth
The reaction of the Nazarenes is thoroughly understandable: there is a certain admiration in their recognition of Jesus' powers. At the village school he would have learnt little more than some reading and memorising large portions of the bible. Hence it seems that they were more astonished by his power and authority in teaching than by his miracles themselves. Yet they cannot bring themselves to face the consequences of this recognition, so blinded are they by their prejudices of what he *should be*. And for this reason Jesus does not work miracles among them, since they would not see that they were signs of a supernatural reality in their midst.

The 'brothers of Jesus' have provided a celebrated point of controversy between confessions, many protestants maintaining that the expression designates 'brothers' in the modern sense of the word. In fact both Greek and semitic words behind it may mean 'close relations'.

What would the reaction be if a prophet appeared in the modern world? How would we judge someone to be a prophet? Who might count as one in recent times?

Mt 14:1–12. Herod and John the Baptist

The Jewish historian Josephus tells us that Herod had the Baptist executed for fear of his popularity and potential for stirring up revolution. The evangelists give a quite different but not necessarily incompatible picture, disregarding political issues and concentrating on personal drama in a way typical of popular stories about the private lives of the great. Mark shows a certain sympathy for Herod, stressing that he had an affection and respect for the Baptist but was forced into his action by feminine scheming. Matthew as usual cuts out all but the essentials of Mark's lively banqueting scene, reduces Herod's vestigial good qualities to vanishing point, and stresses that he knew well that the Baptist was not only 'a good and holy man' but a prophet. For him the Baptist's death stands in the long line of murders of the prophets which will culminate in Jesus' death.

What evils would a modern John the Baptist decry?

Mt 14:13–21. Feeding of the five thousand

This is one of the richest of all the miracle stories. Obviously for the early christians the scene was full of significance as a foretaste of the eucharist, in which Jesus amid his disciples provides himself as food for them.

John's gospel brings out this significance by means of the great discourse on the bread of life; but the other three gospels also show themselves to be aware of it by their wording, which closely echoes that of the narrative of the institution of the eucharist at the last supper.

But the story also looks back to the old testament, showing that Jesus' miracle of providing food for his followers stands in a long tradition—but with points of difference. The most familiar example of this was Moses, who provided manna in the desert (whence Matthew points out that Jesus' miracle occurred 'in a desert place'); the Jews expected that when the messiah came the wonders of the exodus would be renewed, as signs of God's presence among his people. But the closest parallel to the gospel scene is that of Elisha's miraculous feeding of a hundred men with twenty loaves in 2 Kgs 4:42–44; Jesus' miracle is closely modelled, stage by stage, on this, though it is far greater. Jesus' miracle is seen as fulfilling the tradition but breaking its bounds.

Other allusions to Jewish messianic hopes lurk in the story: the green grass, especially in Mark, is an allusion to Ps 23 where the messianic shepherd will feed his flock 'in meadows of green grass'. When Mark mentions specifically groups of fifties and hundreds he is probably alluding to the fact that the people formed the messianic community, for the messianic assembly is prescribed in the documents of Qumran as falling into these divisions.

All this raises the question of how literally factual this account is intended to be. The number of 5,000 seems improbably high at a time when the Roman occupying power was extremely suspicious of messianic, possibly rebellious, groups. It would constitute all the population of a considerable area of sparsely-populated Palestine. Since this miracle may well be identical with the feeding of the four thousand (see below), we may perhaps take the figures to be stylised. Thus many of the details of the story are formed in order to bring out the meaning of the incident for the christian.

Are the evangelists misleading or cheating their readers by using this allusive way of writing? How much do we miss if we fail to understand all the allusions?

Mt 14:22–33. Walking on the water

This incident has many similarities with the calming of the storm in 8:23–27, but here the slight mentions of calming the storm all subserve a different centre of interest. Jesus' coming seems to the disciples like a divine appearance (in the old testament God is several times represented in imaginative language as riding and mastering the waters of chaos), whence their reactions of terror and awe. They are beginning to see Jesus for what he is, and indeed in Matthew's version they finally acknowledge him as 'Son of God'. But it is only to christian ears that this expression implies that Jesus was God, since in the old testament it was used of other persons who were under the special protection of God and had a special mission from him.

Peter's action is typical of his generous and impulsive character (like his actions in Gethsemane and at the high priest's house): he rushes forward and then loses confidence. He is already the leader, but not yet made steady by the advent of the Spirit. He also typifies the disciples at this period of learning, beginning to understand, but still puzzled and fearful.

1. What is the line between trusting and tempting God?

2. How much should we expect extraordinary protection from God in what we try to do for him?

Mt 15:1–20. Traditions of the Pharisees

The full teaching of this passage can be appreciated only by comparison with Mark's version. Mark's version teaches that all the restrictions of the Jewish law concerned with eating are abolished; but Matthew, by rearranging the passage and modifying a few expressions, gives a more restricted lesson, concentrated exclusively on washing the hands (the first and last sentences deal with this point alone). He brings in the passage about honouring father and mother only as part of his argument, to show that some at least of the pharisaic traditions are not to be upheld, as being against the law of God. Then he can go on to say what principles *should* be observed; the sins of his list seem to have in common that they are all sins against one's neighbour. So here again his principle of morality is that of love of the neighbour: it is this alone which determines whether and how the law should be observed; it will be the only standard used at the last judgement. It is because they neglect this that the Pharisees are condemned.

The difference between the two evangelists suggests that each is giving different interpretations of the saying of Jesus on which the passage is centred: 'What goes into the mouth does not make a man unclean; it is what comes out of the mouth that makes him unclean.' In fact the 'apostolic decree' of the council at Jerusalem in Acts 15:29 is dealing with the same question, still enforcing some of the Jewish culinary restrictions on Matthew's own principle of charity to one's neighbour.

The practice to which 15:2–4 refers was that a man could offer to God on their behalf the enjoyment which his parents might have from any debt he owed them, thus absolving himself from allowing them this enjoyment. But at least by the end of the first century AD there were various provisions in the interpretations of the law which protected parents from this hypocritical pseudo-piety.

How much room for diversity, both of practice and of interpretation of the Lord's word, is there within the unity of the church?

Mt 15:21–28. The Canaanite woman

Immediately after this rejection of pharisaic practices comes the contrast of a gentile who shows faith and so wins Jesus' help. The evangelists emphasise that she is not of the chosen race, so has none of the privileges of Israel, none of Israel's claim on God. And Jesus insists that his mission is to Israel. Yet in spite of this it is the pagan woman who accepts Jesus and thereby wrings from him an exception to his practice of directing his mission only to Israel, while those to whom his mission is directed refuse him acceptance.

This passage shows both the power of faith and the singlemindedness with which Jesus concentrated on the conversion of his own people; the exceptional character of this incident proves the rule. It seems that originally he intended that the mission to gentiles should come only afterwards. At this stage he still uses the contemptuous 'dogs' used by Jews to describe gentiles—playfully perhaps, but still unmistakably.

1. *Jesus seems to be hard-hearted at times—is that a characteristic of the gospel?*

2. *Do we think of Jesus as a real person, or as an ideal person?*

Mt 15:28–39. Feeding of the four thousand

This story is in all probability a duplicate of that of the
feeding of the five thousand. Frequently in the old testament two slightly differing accounts of the same incident
are given; it seems as though the compiler never asked
himself the question whether they recounted the same
event, or whether one should be left out. So also Mark
and Matthew; Luke, on the other hand, with some knowledge of the hellenistic conventions which we ourselves
inherit, scrupulously omits what he considers to be dupli-
cates, among them this incident.

Mt 16:1–12. The yeast of the Pharisees and Sadducees

Matthew has altered both these short passages about
Jesus' opponents; he too found them puzzling. According to Mark no sign at all was to be given to the Pharisees
and Sadducees; Matthew does at least allow them the sign
of Jonah, meaning the resurrection (compare 12:40).
The difficulty is that Jesus' miracles were undoubtedly
signs, signs that the kingdom of the messiah had come;
how then can Jesus refuse them any signs? Perhaps what
he means is that there are to be no cosmic portents, such
as were expected to usher in the final renewal of the
world by the messiah. The signs Jesus gives are less
flashy; they do not compel a bemused and dazzled acceptance, as would 'stars crashing from heaven', for it requires
a certain goodwill and attunement already to Jesus to
recognise his miracles as the signs they are.

The next saying, about the yeast, provoked different
treatment from each evangelist, but to each it seemed
puzzling. Mark makes no attempt to explain it, and
makes the disciples' failure to understand it the last in-

stance of their obtuseness before the revelation of Jesus' messiahship. Luke interprets the yeast as hypocrisy, which he considers the Pharisees' worst failing. Matthew interprets it of their teaching; but what particular point on which they agreed does he mean? Could the original saying have taken 'yeast' in the same sense as in the parable of the yeast, and so meant that the disciples were not to be ineffective yeast like the Jewish leaders, who failed to leaven the whole people in preparation for Jesus?

What is this 'good faith' which the Pharisees lacked? What are the prerequisites for accepting the gospel? How can we lead others best to the faith? Why should we?

Mt 16:13–20. Peter's profession of faith

This scene is one of the great turning-points of the gospel; at last one of the disciples responds to Jesus' challenge by acknowledging him as the messiah. So concludes the first stage in the instruction of the apostles; but immediately the second stage begins, for Jesus begins to show what it means to be messiah or to be his follower. The twelve may not reveal that Jesus is the messiah until they have fully understood in what sense he accepts this title, for without the preaching of the cross their message would be deformed.

Matthew has here grouped together a number of sayings of Jesus to Peter—whose semitic form guarantees their antiquity—most of which occur scattered in different places and in slightly different form in the other gospels. This collection is recognised to constitute a passage crucial for any doctrine of church authority; but too often it has also been treated as though the Lord had packed into it, well-hidden though they may be, the answers to a number of questions which could be raised only after considerable development and growth in the christian community.

Even in Mark's version, where Jesus makes no reply at all to Peter, Peter is clearly the leader and spokesman of the disciples—as also elsewhere. But in Matthew Jesus' reply makes this position clearer. Jesus acknowledges Peter's initiative by giving him the special name of 'Rock', himself interpreting this name as signifying the solidity and unshakability of the church which is to be built upon him. Matthew has already used this image of a house built upon rock, contrasting it with impermanence of a house built upon sand (7:24–27). Peter has, then, in the christian church the position which Abraham had in judaism, the 'rock from which Israel was hewn'. The first statement concerns chiefly the church and its indefectibility, drawn from its foundation on rock; only in the second do we hear of jurisdiction. All power of administration in the kingdom of heaven is given to Peter, for the image of giving keys signifies this, both in ancient and in modern times: more particularly, in the semitic world it was used of the appointment of a bailiff or major-domo, who would conduct affairs in his master's name. The final statement about binding and loosing expands this by means of a saying which, in chapter 18, is used to give the same power to the christian community as a whole: its decisions will stand in God's sight, and so have absolute validity. It is highly significant that it is as spokesman of the apostles that Peter is given his powers, and that his power of making binding decisions (but not his position as rock of foundation) is later given also to the whole community.

1. In the modern world with its wider education, how much do we need guidance from the church? Does it not infringe our liberty?

2. *The church cannot fail or change out of all recognition. But how far can it change? What elements are essential to its continuity?*

Mt 16:21-28. The first prophecy of suffering

Now that his position as messiah is firmly recognised Jesus immediately begins to stress that he is no conquering liberator but a servant who must suffer. The first of three predictions of his passion and resurrection is placed here, the first clear mention of the event which is to cast a deepening shadow over the second half of the gospel. The number three itself suggests that these predictions are somewhat stylised expressions of Jesus' knowledge of his impending suffering; the same is suggested by the increasingly exact details. There is no real reason to suppose that the evangelist invented these prophecies, for there are enough veiled hints and allusions in Jesus' other sayings to show that he was in fact aware that he was to suffer execution; this knowledge is indeed the backcloth of his whole message.

After Jesus' prophecy of his own passion come three sayings in which he teaches that his followers must imitate him in this. In fact more is demanded of the disciples even than to lay down their lives in imitation of their master, for in Aramaic 'self' and 'soul' or 'life' are the same word. So what is demanded is that a man should entirely give up himself for Christ's sake in order to find his true self. But Jesus promises that they will begin to find their reward even within this generation, for in one sense the coming of the Son of Man is at the resurrection when the last times of the kingdom begin, and the church is on the straight road to its final fulfilment.

1. How far should we take this 'denying of self'? Should we always do what we dislike doing? Are there always crosses in our way whether we like it or not?

2. How can we give up our selves? Does Jesus demand that we surrender our personalities?

Mt 17:1–8. The transfiguration

Hardly has Jesus begun in earnest to teach the apostles about his suffering than he allows them as a counter-weight to see him as he will be in glory. This experience is to sustain them through the dark hours of the passion, for it is the same three apostles, Peter, James and John, who are to see him on another hillside in his agony before the passion; it will be in different circumstances that he comes to rouse them then. The scene is not without its difficulties. Some hold that it really occurred after the resurrection and has been transferred here, on the grounds that it would be inconsistent with Jesus' full humanity were he suddenly to allow his divinity to shine through; for it is as a supernatural figure that he is repre-sented, and the disciples' fear is awe at a supernatural vision. If this contention is correct the transference itself is significant: the evangelists mean to show that even in his humiliation as man he still remains God.

Another difficulty is to decide in what the actual phenomena consisted. Did his clothes really become sud-denly white? Did two other figures appear, and how were they identified? How could his face shine like the sun? The absurdity of asking this last question literally opens the way to a solution. As 'beaming with pleasure' is a perfectly intelligible expression to us nowadays, so to the early christians, nurtured on the bible, this description would be intelligible in the light of old testament accounts of the appearance of heavenly messengers, particularly in the later prophets. In any case one cannot ask a mystic or visionary who attempts to describe what he has seen: 'But what was actually *there?*' As the voice from the cloud, picking up again the words spoken at Jesus' baptism, shows, it was particularly an experience of his divine commission to teach.

The function of Moses and Elijah has puzzled scholars. In Luke's account they are talking to Jesus about the passion, thus reinforcing the overall sense of the passage. Traditionally they are understood to be representing the support of the law and the prophets for Jesus' message. Perhaps these two figures are chosen because they too were granted a sensible vision of the divine majesty.

What is the difference between a mystical experience and a delusion? How can one distinguish in practice?

Mt 17:9–13. The question about Elijah

Matthew treats this little dialogue as an appendix to the scene of the transfiguration (the mention of Elijah perhaps occasioned its insertion here). Jesus means that John the Baptist was the last of the prophets who was to prepare for the coming of the Lord himself. But the whole passage hints strongly at Jesus' own death: as they rejected and killed his precursor, so will they reject and kill the one whom John foretold.

Mt 17:14–23. The epileptic demoniac

While Mark has a lively and detailed story which fully describes the symptoms of epilepsy in the boy, Matthew is less interested in the miracle as such than in the lesson that faith in Jesus wins healing and that the reason for the disciples' inability to cure the boy was their lukewarm faith. So he cuts down the story to its bare essentials, and replaces Mark's conclusion about the necessity of prayer with a saying (recorded elsewhere in Mark) about the power of the prayer of faith. Jesus' promise seems to be a slippery one in practice: if what we pray for does not happen, then we say retrospectively that we cannot have had as much faith as we thought. Perhaps a solution is that what is at issue is not so much faith as complete trust in Jesus' power and will to help in his own way.

1. What is the answer to the prayer, asked in faith, which yet seems unanswered?

2. Why does Jesus again complain of living among this evil generation, if he fully knows what kind of death is in store for him?

Mt 17:24–27. The temple tax
The temple tax was paid annually by all adult male Jews. Jesus' point is that he and his followers are sons of him to whom the tribute is paid (God) much more intimately than the rest. But he follows this up with the lesson found so prominently in Paul: one must not stand on one's rights of exemption if this will lead others into sin—the lesson of love.

The little story ends with an episode which constitutes one of the most puzzling of Jesus' miracles. The motif of finding a precious object in a fish's mouth is widespread in ancient literature; in Greek literature the story of Polycrates' ring is well known, but in Jewish literature too there are stories of pearls being found in fishes' mouths. This does not mean necessarily that the episode did not happen, but it does make it possible that an element of folklore has crept in.

How far does the gospel accept current thought-forms and modes of expression? How far should we today?

9

Teaching about the community
Mt 18:1–35

The fourth 'book' of Matthew's gospel, concerned with
the special training of the disciples, concludes with a
chapter in which sayings concerning conduct in the community, especially by the leaders of it, are collected.

Mt 18:1–4. Who is the greatest?
The keynote is given by the first little scene: the follower
of Christ must humble himself to become like a child.
But what aspect of a child's attitude is meant? Certainly
nothing sentimental is intended, for Matthew cuts out
the embrace which Jesus gives the child in Mark's version. And he is well aware that there will be sins and
faults in the community, so that he cannot mean the
supposed sinlessness of children. The element which
runs through this whole chapter is the dependence and
receptivity of children. In the passages which follow the
hundredth sheep is lost and must receive help, the debtor
has absolutely no means of his own. This is, then, another
side of that attitude of complete trust and confidence in
the heavenly Father on which Jesus insists so much, the
willingness to be helped and to receive everything from
him.

1. What is true humility? How does it differ from humbug? Are we really meant to be passive, without initiative? Are children?

2. Are children less sinful than adults? Do most people get progressively more sinful?

Mt 18:5–9. Scandal

The first of the three sayings on giving scandal links on to the passage about children. Obviously a danger consequent on this attitude of openness and dependence is that those who have it will be led astray. A *scandalon* ('an obstacle to bring down') is really a trap, such as the spring-board of a mouse-trap.

The other two sayings are linked to the first by the notion of 'scandal'. The last sentiment is so important that Matthew used it also in 5 : 29–30. For all that we would not think of applying it literally. Was this manner of expressing it simply an energetic semitic way of talking, or is it meant literally in a society where maiming and loss of limbs was much more common than in modern society?

Mt 18:10–22. The stray sheep and other sayings

The rest of the chapter is concerned with forgiveness, perhaps the virtue most frequently needed in a community. In the first passage, the parable of the stray sheep, the first lesson is taught, that none of the brethren must ever be written off. Luke's version of the lost sheep (Matthew's change to a 'stray' underlines the remediability of the situation) concentrates on the joy which the recovery of the sheep occasions in heaven, justifying Jesus' association with sinners. But the framework and context here show that Matthew is directing the lesson towards the leaders of the community who are to act as shepherds; their sole task is to bring their charges to God and save them from straying.

Next we are taught the absolute validity of a community decision by the church (15–18) and the reason for it (19–20), Christ's presence in the community. The matter actually in hand should be described not as the legal processes leading to excommunication (the same steps as are prescribed for the Qumran community in the Dead Sea scrolls), but as successive attempts to bring about reconciliation between brethren. The power of binding and loosing here given to the community is the same as that given to Peter in 16:19 and to the apostles in Jn 20:23; it is, then, a power which is inherent in the church by reason of Christ's abiding presence in it, but which may be exercised by the leaders. Christ's real presence in the church is an important element in the evangelist's thinking: as at the beginning he points out that the name 'Emmanuel' means 'God with us', so he concludes with Christ's promise to stay always with the church. Christ's presence in his individual members forms the basis also for the last judgement scene.

Finally the little dialogue with Peter. Seven is to the Hebrews the number of completeness, so to forgive a man seven times means to give unlimited forgiveness. Even this is not enough for Jesus, who increases it to seventy-seven times (or perhaps seventy times seven).

1. What kinds of thing must we forgive in each other? What about each others' national characteristics, temperament, etc?

2. What does Jesus' attitude teach us with regard to the relationship between the church community and its leaders? Should there be such a thing as excommunication in the church?

Mt 18:23–35. Parable of the unforgiving debtor

Matthew likes to finish his collections of sayings (chapters
10, 24–25) with a parable which rounds off and sums up
the collection. There is often, as here, a note of warning
in these parables. It is significant that to conclude his
collection on fraternal relationships he chooses a parable
on forgiveness. The contrast between the behaviour of
the king and that of the servant whom he forgives is
made greater by the absolute impossibility of his ever
repaying the debt. The fellow servant might well have
repaid a hundred denarii (wages for a mere four months
of casual labour), but ten thousand talents represents six
hundred thousand times that sum, over £3 million or
$9 million, a sum which no royal minister could ever
repay. Human forgiveness can be no more than a pale
reflection of the divine forgiveness of a debt which could
never conceivably be paid.

*1. If we can never repay the debt we owe God, that is
just a fact. What conceivable difference can it make to
us?*

*2. What sort of psychological attitude does true for-
giveness involve? When should one not forgive?*

10
The presage of suffering
Mt 19:1–23:39

As the passion approaches Matthew begins the last of his five 'books', into which Jesus' ministry is divided, by passages which show the cost of following Christ. The link which binds these passages together is suffering, restraint, renunciation and service.

Mt 19:1–15. Divorce, celibacy and children
Against the background of rabbinic disagreement about what constituted sufficient grounds for divorce the principle on which Jesus is working is clear: the union of man and wife is of its nature permanent. He reaffirms the teaching of Genesis. In Matthew, it is true, there is a restrictive clause, 'I am not speaking of fornication', about whose meaning no agreement seems possible. Does it mean that remarriage after adultery is permissible (the classic protestant view)? That separation is permissible on the grounds of adultery, but this does not legitimise remarriage (the classic catholic view)? Or does Matthew, who alone has the clause, envisage a particular case not envisaged by the others, namely that of converts from paganism who were already married within the judaeo-christian forbidden degrees (this is a possible meaning of the word translated 'fornication') and must now separate?

Recently the whole question has been given a new turn. Jesus of course condemns the putting asunder of man and wife. But he condemns also, and in the sermon on the mount alongside the condemnation of divorce in Mt 5:32, swearing and revenge. The question is whether, once the failure has occurred and the marriage *de facto* broken up, the church may officially recognise this situation and so allow remarriage, or whether Christ's words forbid this. Paul certainly allows recognition in one class of cases (1 Cor 7:12–15); why is this class different from others?

The passage about 'eunuchs for the sake of the kingdom of heaven' introduces a third new class of eunuchs over those recognised by rabbis. This is traditionally understood as containing the counsel of celibacy. It cannot be understood as counselling castration, since this is included in the second class, 'eunuchs made so by men'; it must refer to the use of marriage. Voluntary celibacy was not regarded as an ideal by the Jews, and was introduced into the Western world by Jesus. The only precedent for it was the prophet Jeremiah, who remained celibate as a witness to the approaching destruction and exile of Judah, which would make having children seem vain.

Finally Jesus' teaching on family life is rounded off by his blessing on children. Probably Matthew does not understand 'children' here in a spiritual sense, since he carefully cuts out the verse in Mark which would suggest this, and transfers it to another position (18:3).

1. Is it possible these days, with our knowledge of human psychology, to accept Jesus' teaching on the permanency of marriage?

2. Would it be more in accordance with human needs

if marriage were for a limited period? Would this be acceptable to christians?

3. What is the point of virginity? Is it not downright unnatural?

Mt 19:16–30. Renunciation and its reward

This passage about the rich young man has always been regarded as the basis for the counsel of poverty in religious orders. But Matthew is more precise; the reason which his version gives for the renunciation is not merely to free the possessor but positively to benfit the poor. He sums up the list of commands given in Mark (already concerned exclusively with duties to our neighbour) by adding 'you must love your neighbour as yourself'. Similarly when he adds 'if you wish to be perfect' one must think of the only other passage where he uses this expression, 5:48, summing up Christ's new law with the command to be perfect 'as your heavenly Father is perfect', who gives with equal generosity to all men. For Matthew, then, poverty is a means to help those who need help, not a perfection in itself.

In this story it is remarkable that the man, who makes his own approach to Jesus, does not follow him in the end. Is it intentional that Jesus himself calls those who become his disciples, and without this initiative on his part there is no discipleship?

It has been pointed out that the sayings on the difficulty of entering the kingdom (24–26) which follow the story would run more smoothly if they contained no reference to wealth; this would better account for the disciples' horror—they had, after all, left everything— and their question in verse 25. Jesus would originally have said that entry into the kingdom was possible for any man only through the gift of God, and the conversation was accommodated to the similar saying about wealthy men in verse 23.

The evangelist concludes by returning to the subject of renunciation and adding a saying on its reward: in the transformation at the dawning of the new era there will be a complete reversal of situation when the followers of Christ receive many times what they renounced. What they receive is expressed in material terms, since this was—and perhaps is still—the only forceful way of expressing prosperity, but obviously the details will not work out; what is meant is the happiness derived from these things. Matthew seems to make a deliberate change to Mark's version; in Mark the reward will be 'now in this present time', but Matthew purposely puts it off till the moment of transformation of the world, by inserting 19: 28 and omitting Mark's phrase. Perhaps Mark's phrase indicates that the last times have already started, and Matthew sees them as delayed; perhaps Matthew is, as elsewhere, making use of the picture of a great universal judgement scene; perhaps he is merely less optimistic.

1. To what extent must all christians embrace Christ's poverty? How poor is this?

2. Can we follow Christ for the sake of the reward? Is this psychologically possible?

Mt 19:30–20:16. Parable of the labourers in the vineyard

By framing the parable with the saying on the first and the last, Matthew shows that he added it here because he understood it to illustrate that lesson. In fact this cannot have been the original lesson of the parable, since the reversal in the chronological order of payment is a minor element quite without theological importance.

More important, and still relevant to Matthew's immediate point of reward by God, is the generosity of the owner. But to discover the original sense of a parable we must look for the element which is naturally central in the story; in this case it seems to be the complaints of the earlier workers and their rebuke as ungenerous. As the original context of the parable one might, then, reconstruct some such scene as is recorded in Mt 9:10–13: Jesus offers salvation to sinners, and those who have long observed the law object that they have earned more. There is, however, the same reward of eternal life offered to all, regardless of their earning-power, which therefore comes to seem rather irrelevant. The specific context of those who observe the old law is suggested by the figure of a vineyard which, since Is 5:1–7, inevitably suggested to a Jew the vineyard of the Lord, which is Judah and Jerusalem.

But isn't this unfair? What about the value of our good works? Are we to be no better off?

Mt 20:17–28. Third prophecy of suffering

Once again Jesus' prediction that he is to suffer and die is followed by the lesson that his followers must share his suffering. The disciples still had not understood that participation in his kingdom means participating also in his passion, and were thinking only of sharing his final glory. To spare James and John the brunt of the blame for this, Matthew puts the question (spoken by them in Mark) into their mother's mouth.

In describing his suffering Jesus uses two figures which show his understanding of its nature as expiating the sins of others: a cup is used often in the old testament as a symbol for God's retribution for sin and similarly baptism

in the new testament is always a rite of purification
for sin. Jesus' suffering, therefore, purifies from sin and
does away with its punishment. Jesus is fully aware of
what is to come and goes forward with his eyes open.
Finally he gives what is perhaps the fullest expression in
the synoptic gospels of his mission of service, the lesson
which he gives in the fourth gospel in dramatic form by
washing the disciples' feet. In both cases he emphasises
that this is only an example to be followed by christian
leaders, whose glory is not to be honoured but to serve.

*Suffering and sickness are (theoretically) all very well
for christians, but what of others who do not understand
them: how are they not an argument against God's existence?*

Mt 20:29–34. Two blind men of Jericho

This last of Jesus' cures seems at first out of place here
at the final stage of preparation for the passion. But its
position is highly significant: the opening of the blind
men's eyes symbolises the opening of the eyes of the
world when Jesus publicly manifests himself at Jerusalem, as he is about to do; thanks to their faith they see
the salvation of God; but at Jerusalem men refuse him
faith and reject him.

*As the scene is presented (which, remember, is all we
have to go on), was it the constant nagging of the blind
men which won them Jesus' attention? Or is the point of
the story somewhere else?*

Mt 21:1–17. The messiah enters Jerusalem and the temple

Jesus' Jerusalem ministry now begins with a solemn
entry into the city and a purification of the temple. In

fact the Jerusalem ministry as presented by the first three gospels is probably a collection of events which took place on various occasions. Some of the incidents (the four controversies: 22: 14–46) are clearly artificially brought together, and in general the pace of development of events is improbably rapid. The evangelist gives, then, a review of Jesus' ministry in Jerusalem, which finally led to his arrest and rejection by the leaders of the people, in the dramatic form of a stay of a few days.

The preface to this chapter is provided by the messianic entry. Jesus' entry into Jerusalem on a feast day with his disciples was the fulfilment of the prophecies and is described as such. Indeed its meaning, or the deeper reality of it, are so prominent that what actually occurred rather falls into the background. To begin with, Matthew systematically exaggerates the element of crowd participation; where Mark's account has 'many people' Matthew makes it 'a very great crowd'; where Mark has 'those who went in front' Matthew gives 'the crowds which went in front'; finally 'the whole city was in turmoil' has no justification in Mark's account which Matthew is clearly drawing upon as a basis for his version. The numbers remain vague, but the impression is given of a great public manifestation, although Mark's version is quite compatible with the simple arrival of Jesus and his disciples among other pilgrims.

The green branches and the acclamations from Ps 118 are features of the Jewish feasts of tabernacles and the dedication of the temple. The latter feast would have been a most suitable occasion for this entry of Jesus, for it commemorated the purification and rededication of the temple after its defilement by the Greeks in 167 BC, an event which was considered to be the establishment of a new era. Jesus' action is closely parallel to this. But the evangelists clearly understand the cries and gestures as being directed—consciously or unconsciously—to Jesus.

To the strictly 'objective' historian this procedure might seem unjustified. But the evangelists make no claim to be strictly objective or to relate the bare bones of events (nor, for that matter, does any historian worth the name; even selection, let alone ways of describing events, is necessarily interpretative). They write for believers and describe the events as they acually took place, but bringing out their significance and interpreting them as they appear to the eyes of faith.

The clue to the whole scene in the evangelists' minds is the verse of Zechariah which Matthew quotes. This is the prophetic prediction whose fulfilment gives the event its significance. There was a rabbinic tradition that, if Israel was unworthy to receive the messiah in the triumphant form which was generally awaited, he would come thus in humility on a donkey. And for Matthew especially Jesus is the humble king—'learn of me for I am gentle and humble in heart'.

Immediately after this entry, according to Matthew (Mark leaves it till the next day, but Matthew heightens the dramatic effect) Jesus goes to the temple and symbolically purifies it and inaugurates the final messianic era. The tremendous significance of this event is lost without knowledge of the old testament background. Malachi had prophesied: 'The Lord you are seeking will suddenly enter his temple . . . he is like the refiner's fire . . . he will purify the sons of Levi' (3 : 1–3). Zechariah had promised that on the day on which the Lord came to Jerusalem from the Mount of Olives (like Jesus) to be declared king over all nations there, 'there will be no more traders in the temple of Yahweh Sabaoth when that day comes'

(14:21). It is this scriptural background rather than the moral depravity of dealers in the temple which gives the scene its sense, for there is no evidence or hint that their trade was in itself reprehensible. The sacrificial victims must be purchased and the various local coinages exchanged (a reasonable four per cent was charged) into the stable currency of Tyrian silver used for the temple. The two scriptural quotations in 21:13 in their own contexts do not make a contrast between prayer and robbery, but both refer to the acceptability of sacrifices, which depends on Israel's fidelity to the covenant; so Jesus is, in this way too, alluding to the fact that he is establishing a new covenant whose temple and sacrifice are perfectly acceptable.

Jesus has inaugurated a new order which we enjoy. Are there any factors in our contemporary church and world which Jesus might also justifiably rebel against, as he did in fulfilling the old testament prophecies? Do we bring a new era into operation in any sphere of life by following Jesus?

Mt 21:18–22. The barren fig-tree

It was only the cripples and children who acknowledged Jesus in the temple; the people, as represented by their leaders, were merely indignant. So, by a prophetic action reminiscent of the old testament prophets, Jesus signifies that Israel, barren and unfruitful, is to wither. This action would be readily intelligible because Israel had been likened by Jeremiah (8.13) to a fig-tree upon which God seeks fruit in vain.

1. Why is it that our prayers seem to be answered so seldom?

2. Haven't fig-trees any rights?

Mt 21:23–27. A challenge to Jesus' authority

This passage begins the final show-down between Jesus and the regular authorities of the Jews. It is a conflict between charismatic and hierarchical authority, for they approach Jesus to ask on what authority he is teaching, since a rabbi had his authority to teach from his own rabbi, who ordained his pupil and empowered him to teach in his turn by imposition of hands. They ask, in effect, what rabbi had so ordained him. He throws back the challenge by asking whether John the Baptist, who had been recognised by the people as having charismatic or prophetic authority, not ordained and hierarchical, had been duly ordained. By their refusal to answer, the leaders show that they are too narrow, refusing in the teeth of popular recognition to accept that there could be any special authority from God which breaks through their orderly categories. Granted this refusal, they are incapable of allowing that God could make any intervention in human affairs such as the renewal and transformation expected of the messiah.

1. Should only ordained ministers teach and preach?
2. What part has a 'John the Baptist' type figure to play in the modern church? What sort of authority have such prophetic figures?

Mt 21:28–22:14. Four parables

Of these four parables the first three are directed against the leaders of the Jews. They form a collection by Matthew from various sources, inserted here by the evangelist. The first is so matthean in style and vocabulary that it is clear that he received it from oral tradition and first put it in writing himself. The second is derived from Mark, slightly embroidered. The third is shared by Luke, and probably derives from the collection of sayings of Jesus which these two evangelists both used. The last is not in any other gospel but has a very close parallel in a parable told by Rabbi Johanan ben Zakkai, a contemporary of Matthew; from a historical and literary point of view it is possible, though unprovable, that Matthew himself added this parable to the gospel tradition to illustrate the message of Jesus. Certainly not every detail of the parables derives from Jesus himself.

The parable of the two sons is explicitly directed against the leaders of the Jews who claim to do God's will by their adherence to the law, contrasting them with sinners who make no such claim. Its original context could well have been, like the parable of the labourers in the vineyard, a situation where Jesus is explaining why he consorts with moral outcasts of the Jewish world.

The parable of the wicked husbandmen provokes the Pharisees to a response, not that of conversion but that of sanguinary opposition. They could not mistake that it was directed at themselves, since the vineyard is so clearly Israel (as in Is 5, with which Jesus opens), and they are the official stewards of Israel's heritage. In the form given by Matthew the parable is a transparent allegory, in which the two groups of messengers are the earlier and later prophets sent to warn Israel. The beloved son could be understood as Jesus even though no claim to be Son of God in the sense understood by christians was perceived, for in Jewish terminology any special messenger of God could be described as a son of God. Matthew develops a mere hint of Mark's and adds another saying (21 : 43) to include more positive teaching: not only will the vineyard be taken away from the charge of the Pharisees; it will be entrusted to others who will produce its fruit. Matthew thus envisages the situation of the church, whereas Mark stops at the failure of the Jewish nation. Between the two expansions which contain this teaching Matthew includes the saying about the corner-stone; of this new people which holds the vineyard Christ is the key-stone.

The parable of the invitation to a wedding feast is also greatly allegorised to bring out its meaning, as appears from a comparison with Luke's version. For Matthew the central point is that the Jews refuse to come into the kingdom and it therefore passes to others. The meaning is made clearer by the change of a banquet in the original story into a king's wedding feast for his son—the messianic age is often described in terms of a wedding feast. And the worthlessness of the invited guests is emphasised: they do not even bother to make excuses, as in Luke, but simply go off 'uninterested'; they quite gratuitously maltreat the messengers (in the previous parable the husbandmen had some cause for this, but the guests have none). Correspondingly their punishment is stressed; in Luke they are merely left out of the banquet, but in Matthew their city is burnt.

The final parable of the wedding garment is really separate from the previous story, and is a warning in turn to those who do accept the invitation. We are constantly reminded in Matthew that the church contains both good and bad elements which have yet to be separated. In Johanan ben Zakkai's similar parable the white garment stands for good works, so it may be that the lesson of this parable is that mere membership of the church, without the works of love, is unavailing.

1. What would be modern parallels to each of the attitudes shown by these four parables?

2. *Is pride really the worst of the sins which prevent our entering the kingdom?*

Mt 22:15–46. Four controversies

Another collection now shows the parting of the ways between Jesus and each of the four leading parties of the Jews. Matthew emphasises that they have no wish to learn from him by their questions but only to catch him out, until finally Jesus himself puts a question, reflection on which might lead them a long way to recognising his full dignity.

The question on tribute to Caesar confronts the Pharisees and the Herodians (possibly a patriotic party which wanted independence from Rome and the Herod family back on the throne). There might well be discussion between them on the point of paying tribute, for the Pharisees advocated obedience in all things to the occupying power, whereas the Herodians may have advocated civil disobedience to gain independence. So if they turned to Jesus to resolve their dispute it would not necessarily be from malice towards him; perhaps this interpretation is a later addition, made at a time when the political background had been forgotten. In any case Jesus cuts through their quarrel to a more important principle. He is clearly not interested in the political issue, for he makes no attempt to assess *what* belongs to Caesar, and lays the whole weight on the second phrase of his answer. But circumstances of Judaea at the time of Christ were so different from those of the modern world that it would be quite unjustified to conclude from Jesus' lack of participation in politics that the christian has no part to play in them.

The question on resurrection brings on to the stage the

Sadducees, the conservative, aristocratic, priestly families, who refused to accept not only resurrection but other more recent developments in theology, such as those about angels. Their question is obviously framed to ridicule the belief. Jesus gives two replies, of which the former is both clearer and more important: their idea of the afterlife as a continuation of the more pleasurable elements in this life is misconceived. It is impossible to conceive, still less imagine, what the joys of eternal life will be, since we cannot realise what is meant by the transformation which takes place at the glorification of our bodies. Even Paul can only stutter and use analogies (1 Cor 15: 35–53). Jesus' latter argument is a rabbinic scriptural one, of less interest to us: God is a living, acting, saving God, and if Abraham, Isaac and Jacob are no more, he has not saved them.

The last question to Jesus comes from a lawyer; in Mark he seems well disposed, and is congratulated for his answer by Jesus, but in Matthew he has taken on the venom of the Pharisees. The background to the question is the dispute among lawyers as to which of the 613 commandments of the law were great, and which small. But Jesus' answer is striking for its novelty. As usual he cuts through to essentials and gives the principle which lies behind all the 613 commandments. Unasked he adds the second to the first and unprecedentedly claims that all revelation can be derived from these. Matthew insists that the two commands are on the same level, an insistence shocking to the Jews for whom religion had become ever more concerned with rites and reverence paid to a remote and awesome deity, and ever less concerned with relationships of love between men. One of the most prominent features of Matthew is a care to redress this balance. John would go even further, and say that the two commandments are in fact one; it would be false to suppose that part of the law and the prophets derives from one, part from the other, for the whole derives from them both, from the first through the second.

Finally Jesus himself poses a conundrum about the messiah: he is descended from David but greater than he. It is remarkable, in view of the christian habit of referring simply to 'Christ', how reticent Jesus was with regard to this title; in the synoptic gospels he uses it extremely rarely, and in John not at all. Similarly the title 'Son of David' occurs very seldom except in Matthew. This is because both titles were heavy with political overtones, for every movement of rebellion against Rome claimed that its leader was messiah. A great part of Jesus' teaching, for example the parables of the kingdom, is concerned to correct this conception, but it was through skilful manipulation of the association of the ideas of messiah and rebellion that he was finally condemned.

1. What duty have christians to engage in politics?
2. What will heaven be like?
3. Can love of God and neighbour be opposed? Where the points of view expressed by Matthew and by John are clearly different (though each claims the support of Jesus) how do we resolve the problem?

Mt 23:1–39. Hypocrisy of the scribes and Pharisees

The scribes and Pharisees represent the religious teachers of the Jews. Scribes were professional interpreters of the law, learned in the traditions and opinions of the various schools of interpretation, men with memories trained to remember the case-law constituted by previous decisions, and so interpret the will of God for any situation which arose. The Pharisees were not professional scholars but formed a loose party of those who set out to observe the law in its entirety, drawn from many classes and professions; some were priests, others lawyers, others craftsmen or (like Paul) tent-makers. From their very situation it was inevitable that two sorts of temptation should lie open before them. In interpreting the law, especially so much according to precedent, they would be liable to excessive severity, sticking to principles in disregard of the human situation with which they were dealing. Hence Jesus' central charge against them. The central block of the indictment in this chapter is the sevenfold charge beginning 'Alas for you . . .'; of this the central accusation, and so the centre-point of Jesus' whole indictment, is that they lack discernment and love and good faith. The particular overtones of the word here used for 'love' ('love' is a very general word in English; in Greek there are several words, and this one is especially rich in old testament overtones) are drawn from two special uses of the word. Its common use is for a love which is respectful of but shows pity for the unfortunate; but in biblical language it connotes especially the love which an Israelite owes his kinsman when he is in need, and more particularly the love which binds husband and wife in the marriage contract. Further richness is given by the use of this word for the love which God bears Israel, which causes him to care for, foster, protect and forgive his people. All these aspects of love, rather than unfeeling legalism, the judge and legislator must show, for throughout his gospel Matthew brings out Christ's insistence that love is the only guide-line in the application of law.

The other charges against the scribes and Pharisees are all summed up in the charge of hypocrisy, again a danger inherent in the very situation. They themselves, or the best among them, were well aware of their proneness to this failing, for the later Pharisaic rabbis have left a number of amusing stories against themselves on this count. It is of course a danger which faces any who profess a religious way of life, any number of failings being concealed on the pretext of a witness to religious values.

The chapter ends with a passage (33–39) which sums up all Jesus' ministry, which is now complete, and his loving attention to the Jews. It remains one of the great mysteries of the gospel how God could have prepared the chosen race so long and so lovingly for the coming of the messiah in whom their history was to culminate, only for them to fail at the moment of decision.

In our 'open' society, in which knowledge and communication are at a premium, is every kind of hypocrisy condemned sufficiently openly? Who are the modern blind guides? Advertisers? Novelists? Film producers?

11

The shape of things to come
Mt 24:1–25:46

The two chapters which follow, and more especially
24: 1–31, are often a source of embarrassment to christians today. It is absurd to suppose that 'the stars will
fall from heaven'; indeed such an expression has hardly
any literal sense for the modern world-picture. To make
matters worse, according to 24:34, this was to happen
within one generation; it did not. Even the scene of the
last judgement cannot be understood in a literal sense
now that we are aware of the countless billions of human-
kind: where would one find room for them all? We must,
however, find some sense for these chapters: it is a mere
subterfuge—and an inept one—to resort to the solution
that these are not the sayings of Jesus but that the evangelist used a Jewish apocalyptic tract. The warmest
partisans of this theory have not succeeded in satisfac-
torily reconstructing this tract, and in any case it is
the gospel as a whole that contains the message of Christ
which we are trying to understand, not merely those parts
of it which contain his words as they were actually
uttered. A christian cannot brush these chapters aside as
visionary distortions born of a curious mentality among
first-century believers.

   But what is the overall message contained in them?
It is clear from the great quotations from Daniel which

occur as milestones in the first part that a symbolic language is being used to describe a great future. From the resemblance to contemporary writings one may deduce that the main purpose is to encourage christians under persecution with the assurance of final victory after great distress. But is any particular event envisaged? The mention of the present generation has led scholars to pinpoint the destruction of Jerusalem in AD 70 as the moment of triumph for christianity, when it was emancipated from judaism and also freed from Jewish persecution (but Acts hardly shows general persecution of the church by Jews before that date). Others have opted for the moment of the resurrection of Christ as the beginning of the triumph of the church, using also the clear expectation among the earliest christians that the last times of the world, inaugurated then, would be of short duration and were soon to be concluded by the return of Christ in glory. Certainly this expectation is evident in these chapters. But since this return did not occur—and already the later Paul and the gospel of John do not consider it an important factor to determine christian attitudes— can we not say that this expectation was misconceived, and that the message of the passage for christians today must be understood by discounting it? Christ was not to return in this way, but rather by the coming of his Spirit at Pentecost.

But this gives rise to further problems. Since the widespread belief among Jews that there would be some sort of cataclysmic event in the near future which would establish the people of God in peace and power was shared by the early christians (whose understanding of who constituted the people of God was nevertheless different), must we not say that Jesus, who drew his mental equipment and psychology from a certain milieu at a certain era, would have expressed and indeed understood his message in similar terms? Here we must grasp firmly the statement which has so long embarrassed theologians, that not even the Son knows the day and the hour of it (24:36). Jesus too, then, could do no more than describe the future glory and ultimate vindication of the church by God in the symbolic terms current in his time, and—on account of their biblical associations —packed with overtones for his contemporaries. It is not necessary to suppose that he had in mind any particular future event in the history of the world (according to Acts 1:7 he did not consider it necessary to know 'times or dates that the Father has decided by his own authority'). Nor should we interpret the passage as though Jesus spoke in deliberately veiled and symbolic terms of precise happenings which he *could* perfectly well have described in 'straightforward' terms. This would be to misunderstand the nature of prophetic utterances, and the purpose at any rate of this prophecy.

Only after these questions have been raised is it profitable to discuss whether in fact we have to do here with the words of Jesus. In its present form the passage is not verbatim from Jesus; the 'let the reader understand' of 24:15 shows that it is essentially a written, not a spoken, piece. It is also different in character from the sayings of Jesus handed down in the first three gospels, for with the exception of the parables, these are all short, pithy pronouncements, almost epigrams of a proverbial and so easily memorable cast, whereas 24:4–31 is one broad development, which would have been much harder to memorise exactly. The word used for the 'coming' of Christ is a typically Greek expression; it was not used by Jesus, but brought into christian usage by Paul. But a number of sayings of Jesus are surely incorporated in it, for such sayings are recorded in other parts of the gospel (eg 19:29–30), which shows that Jesus must have spoken about the future.

The technique used by the so-called apocalyptic writings of later judaism, whose style has such analogies with the style of this passage, was to describe in the form of a vision, usually granted to a distinguished Jewish historical figure, the sufferings and persecution which the chosen people were undergoing at the time of writing. Then came a prophecy of deliverance and triumph over the persecutor. Two examples of such are Dan 7–12, and the Revelation of John. The difference between the Jewish and the christian apocalyptic writing is that the final cataclysm which liberates and establishes the elect is described in terms, no longer of a visitation by God, but of a visitation or coming of Christ (this parallel is itself instructive, for the idea of some visible coming of God is surely absurd: should not one then understand the visible coming of Christ as being a naive description of what is in fact less material?). Mark's apocalypse (13:1–37) follows this pattern fairly clearly: there is a crescendo of suffering and distress, culminating in cosmic signs and portents and the coming of the Son of Man to gather his chosen ones. Matthew somewhat alters the emphasis: he has moved the passage on persecution to an earlier chapter where Jesus is preparing the disciples for their apostolate, and now his emphasis is more on the danger that 'love in most men will grow cold' (24:12). As time goes on, the first enthusiasm will wane. Matthew has constantly been aware of this danger, and this is why he has so often inserted here and there a word of warning about the coming judgement, the great judgement with the picture of which he concludes this section. This is also why he takes up four sentences of the conclusion of

Mark's apocalyptic chapter (13:33–36) in which Mark warned people to be on the watch and prepared for the end, and inserts a full parable corresponding to each of them (Mt 24:42–25:30): the watchful householder, the conscientious steward, the ten bridesmaids, the talents. In Matthew the lesson of each of these is the same: make use of your time and opportunities while you may, for the final reckoning will come—a moral pointed in the last verse of each.

Christ is the Lord of history: does this mean anything in a world of moon rockets and atom bombs? Is there any way in which we can make the second coming important and meaningful for ourselves?

Mt 25:1–13. The parable of the ten bridesmaids

Of the four parables just mentioned the first two are straightforward enough, but the third is more puzzling than our familiarity with it allows us to think. Firstly, keeping awake is not the virtue required by the story, in spite of 25:13, for even the good five go to sleep; what is required is to be ready and equipped. There is clearly an allegory in which oil in the lamps stands for virtue or good works; this allegory saves the sensible girls from what would otherwise be reprehensible selfishness; but the allegory cannot be pressed too far, for these qualities cannot be bought. The translation 'bridesmaids' is not really fitting, since the girls (literally 'virgins') are attendants not on the bride but on the groom; Palestinian customs were different from ours, seemingly including a torchlight procession to meet the bridegroom as he comes to the marriage-feast; but the expression 'bridesmaids' at least gives the right impression of girl attendants at a wedding.

In what ways must we today be prepared for Christ at all times?

Mt 25:14–30. The parable of the talents

This parable too is heavily allegorised (Luke's version much less so). But again the allegory cannot be pressed too far, for Christ, as the master who comes back for a reckoning, cannot be described as a hard man, reaping where he has not sown; this encourages us to concentrate on the main point of the story, that a reckoning will be asked concerning the good use of capacities and resources in the time allowed to each man. The parable was perhaps originally addressed to the religious leaders of the Jews; they were given a sacred deposit with the task of fostering it by preparing the people for the coming of Christ. This makes sense of the conclusion (25 : 28–29) for, when they failed to lead the people to Christ, they lost even what was valuable in the old law. The same moral is easily transferred to the christian situation.

1. How is a man with less gifts able to avoid being jealous of the man with many?

2. What are the gifts that are important for the kingdom of heaven? How should they be put to use?

Mt 25:31–46. The last judgement

This scene is a supreme example of the use and transformation of Jewish material. The basis is the Jewish idea of a final judgement scene, but there are three major points of difference. In the Jewish scenes it is God who judges: here it is Christ in glory, for Christ's true position in the universe, barely veiled and often showing through in the rest of Matthew, is revealed. In Jewish scenes the gentiles appear, if at all, only to hear their condemnation; here 'all nations' are gathered and judged on an equal footing. Finally the Jewish principle of judgement according to good works is used; but here the criterion is uniquely the good works of love. The whole of Matthew's presentation of morality as being a matter of acting in love culminates here, and the peculiarly christian motive is given: the presence of Christ not only in his church as a whole but in each individual. Can one say that this presence is restricted to members of the church alone? There is certainly no explicit restriction mentioned here.

1. How are we to take Christ's words 'as long as you did it to one of the least of my brethren you did it to me'? Does it apply universally?

2. In what ways can we feed the hungry, clothe the poor, visit the sick, etc? Who are the poor in the twentieth century, anyway?

12

The passion, death and resurrection of Jesus
Mt 26:1–28:20

The effect on the reader of the passion accounts intended by the authors of the first three gospels was not to arouse pity for Jesus, horror at his sufferings or even (directly) remorse for the sins which caused them. Nor did they seek to explain why this particular historical process was chosen by God to bring men to peace with himself. Rather they seek to illustrate, again and again, two key themes of these events: first Jesus was throughout in complete control; his calm mastery of events, his unpretentious but majestic direction of affairs is never more evident than now; he goes forward with clear knowledge of what is to come and unswerving will to achieve it. The second theme in the light of which the evangelists describe events is complementary to the first: these happenings were decreed by God from the beginning; an air of ineluctable destiny hangs over the passion narrative, largely lent by the many scriptural quotations and allusions. For the Jew the scriptures enshrine the testimony of God's will and intentions for man. When, therefore, the early christians were confronted with the scandal of the cross, the incredible paradox that the man they claimed as glorious messiah had fallen victim to the sordid little execution reserved for lower-class petty criminals and malcontents, they could explain this only by referring to the will of God as seen in the scriptures, and of Jesus himself as seen in his foreknowledge and control of events.

Mt 26:1–13. Bethany

Jesus died a criminal's death and received a criminal's burial; but one shame at least he was spared: he was not to be buried unanointed. The horror with which the Jews regarded this disgrace explains the prominence which this passage receives. It also shows Jesus' foreknowledge, outstripping any inkling of his followers; he sees the full significance of a normal act of courtesy to a guest. Immediately the air becomes heavy with the presage of suffering. But why this unprecedented promise to the unnamed woman? Surely her act, lovingly attentive as it was, was not so unique? Was the action of anointing for burial in itself crucial enough to merit a special guarantee of remembrance?

26:11 is frequently used as a justification for lavishing expense on churches and their furnishings, when the same money could bring relief to those in need. Whether such expense is justified or not, this text at least cannot be invoked, since Jesus makes this attention to his body quite unique; afterwards, he points out, the situation will be reversed, and the poor alone remain to merit such attention.

Should we build expensive churches and lavish money on sacramentals, etc, or should we rather help the poor in every possible way?

Mt 26:14–29. The betrayal and last supper

In Mark the preliminaries to the supper are filled with lively details: the delight of the high priests when Judas approaches them, the identification of the owner of the supper-room by means of the odd phenomenon of a man carrying a water-pot (very strange; normally only women would do this). In Matthew these all fade away into the hieratic calm and solemnity of the moment, Jesus in control and mysteriously directing the course of events, Judas unknowingly fulfilling the scriptures in the price he accepts—the sum to be paid in restitution for the accidental death of a slave.

Of the supper itself the account is so condensed that a good deal of background about the paschal meal is presupposed. Of the institution of the eucharist the evangelist hands on only the brief account which was recited in the early church—as the account of the institution is still the central part of the eucharistic prayer today—as warrant of what was done at each celebration of the eucharist. But a great deal of the significance of Jesus' action comes from the paschal context in which it takes place.

The first question to be asked, however, is why Jesus gave his body and blood to be eaten and drunk. The purpose of any sacred meal is to achieve union with the divinity; and this too was the purpose of the sacrificial meals of the old testament. The whole context of the present chapter, and also the single phrase of explanation given by Jesus (my blood 'poured out for many for the forgiveness of sins') show that this action is sacrificial in character—not itself the climax of sacrifice, but intimately connected with it, and part of the whole movement of sacrifice already begun and culminating on the cross. The purpose of the sacrifice is to unite men to God by the abolition of their sins: there can be no more obvious and fuller means by which men can be taken up into this union than by union of themselves, fully and physically

—but not only physically, for 'flesh and blood' embraces the whole person—to the victim, the means of union. This is most strikingly true of the blood, for the blood of a victim might never be consumed by man, since the Hebrews considered it to 'contain' the life, and so belong only to God, the giver of life; by drinking his blood, then, the disciples partake of the life of the victim, divine because it belongs only to God, divine by reason of the person whose blood it is, and salvific because by its outpouring sins are forgiven.

It is also 'the blood of the covenant', and here the paschal context enters in. At the pasch the Jews remembered the deliverance of Israel from slavery to become, by the marriage bond of the old covenant, God's special people; this bond was ratified by the sprinkling of blood over the people. Now Jesus, delivering his followers from the slavery of sin, ratifies a new bond with them by blood, making them a new people of God. This bond will endure for ever, but the eucharist concludes with a sentence whose purpose is surely to direct their gaze towards the final completion.

1. How can we best express and understand our participation in Christ's work of redemption by the eucharist? By symbolic language? By explaining it in terms of human sacrificial actions on behalf of others? How do we ourselves get involved?

2. Is the whole notion of sacrifice too hopelessly primitive to have meaning today? How can its force be got across?

Mt 26:30–56. Gethsemane
The agony in Gethsemane poses in its most acute form the problem of the compatibility of Jesus' divine and

human natures. While remaining God he yet underwent the horror and shrinking natural to man at the prospect of the death he was to undergo (though one may ask to what degree he was aware of its details). This difficulty, the abasement of the majestic Christ, and the unflattering picture of the twelve rule out the possibility that the scene was subsequently invented. On the other hand some of the details may well have been filled out, for the apostles were not near enough to hear Jesus' prayer. The triple occurrence of the prayer may be a literary device, used elsewhere in the gospels, for emphasis. As to its contents, Matthew takes for its climax the phrase of the prayer Jesus taught his disciples: 'Your will be done', thus expressing Jesus' total submission to and trust in the Father. The other important element in the account is the need for Jesus' disciples to join with him in his sufferings by watching and praying, constantly trying again when, through the weakness which their master knows, they fail to live up to their ideals.

The dominant feature of the account of the arrest is that it is carried out entirely under Jesus' direction; only when he gives his permission can it proceed; at any moment could he, in perfect union with the Father, prevent it by overwhelming force—if it were not God's will, as manifested in the scriptures, that it should occur. The proverbial-sounding saying 'all who draw the sword will die by the sword' has become a motto of pacifists. But can it really bear this weight? In its present position it has little weight, for Jesus' refusal to oppose violence with violence is not grounded on disapproval of violence in general, but upon the very special circumstances: the will of the Father that he should be so arrested.

1. How is it possible for Jesus to be at one and the same time so obviously in control of the situation (twelve

legions of angels, 26 : 53) and yet so terrified at the pros-
pect of suffering?

2. Does the gospel help us to see why such ordinary
frail mortals as the apostles were chosen by Jesus to be
his companions?

3. Is soldiering against the spirit of Christ?

Mt 26:57–68. The Jewish interrogation

From a comparison of the various gospel accounts and
from the probabilities of the legal situation at the time
it seems most likely that there was no formal trial of Jesus
by the Jews, but only an interrogation during the night
at the high priest's house, designed to elicit a charge to
bring against Jesus before Pilate, followed by a meeting
of the sanhedrin in the morning to approve the decisions
there made. The charge which they attempt to fasten on
Jesus is that of stirring up revolution—and Jesus was indeed a revolutionary, though not in their sense. Jesus
preserves the dignified silence which is such a feature of
his conduct at the trials; it is so stressed probably because
it fulfils the prophecy of the suffering servant in Is 53 : 7:
'he bore it humbly, he never opened his mouth'. When
finally the high priest challenges him on oath to admit
to being the messiah (which the high priest no doubt
wished to take as evidence of stirring up revolution),
Jesus refuses for this reason to accept the title in the
sense offered: this is the sense of 'The words are your
own'. He then goes on to correct this conception of the
messiah by lifting it above any petty political connotations and linking it to the glorious figure seen by Daniel
in his vision: 'On him was conferred glory and kingship,
and men of all peoples, nations and languages became
his servants' (Dan 7 : 14). Jesus is forced by the high priest
into the fullest statement of his cosmic dominion in the

first three gospels. In what sense they had reason to regard it as blasphemy is disputed; but the fact is that they were determined to find some grounds for accusation. They were preparing to play on Pilate's ignorance of the niceties of Jewish theology, and wilfully to disregard Jesus' careful statement of the nature of his messiahship when they presented the charge of claiming to be king of the Jews. This charge was intended to suggest precisely those politico-revolutionary pretensions which Jesus had just so carefully denied.

It is as a prophet—one of the titles of the messiah—that Jesus is mocked. According to Mark he was blindfolded, so that this would be a game of blind man's bluff, in which he is challenged to name who gave the blow. Matthew suggests that it was the councillors themselves who indulged in this undignified buffoonery; is he deliberately correcting Mark who makes it clear that the attendants were the tormentors?

1. What good would it have done Jesus to show up the accusers as false? Can we say we would have behaved in the way he did? Was there any chance of his escaping death?

2. Under what circumstances should we follow Christ's footsteps, denying our own will and taking the consequences: when should we avoid suffering as an evil?

Mt 26:69–75. Peter's denial
By design Peter's weakness and failure to profess his loyalty to his master, so soon after his protestations of willingness to die for him, are set over against Jesus' own steadfastness. The triple denial emphasises its absoluteness, and what would have been its finality except for Jesus' forgiveness.

1. If Peter had not denied Christ they might have crucified him too. Would that have been the right thing to happen? Isn't it foolish to get oneself martyred?

2. Do we ever deny Christ, eg by keeping silent when a gross injustice occurs? Is that kind of shunning of responsibility unimportant?

Mt 27:1–10. The death of Judas

This passage is full of scriptural overtones drawn confusedly from Jeremiah and Zechariah to interpret the fate of Judas by the scriptures. The account of the same events in Acts 1 shows the same procedure by means of different allusions. The references to Zechariah bring in the idea of the mockery of God and his representative by being valued at such a ludicrously small sum (see Zech 11:4–13). The way in which Judah dies, suicide by hanging, compares him to Ahitophel, who killed himself in the same way after betraying his master David. Finally the potter's quarter, Hakeldama on the slopes of the valley Gehenna, carries with it reminiscences of Gehenna or hell, for it was the refuse dump of Jerusalem, where decay and fires raged continuously.

Judas' motives remain enigmatic. His second name 'Iscariot' probably means 'the treasurer', as we know he was from Jn 12:6, which also says he was a thief. But avarice can hardly have been his only motive; thirty silver pieces is too paltry a sum.

Mt 27:11–26. Jesus before Pilate

To call this passage an account of the trial before Pilate would be incorrect; it is an account of how the leaders of the Jews got Jesus condemned by Pilate. Of the trial all we hear is the charge of being king, which Jesus again accepts only with reserve, and miscellaneous charges to which he maintains his symbolic silence. The rest is an account of Pilate's triple attempt to release Jesus, each time foiled by the Jews at the persuasion of the high priests and elders. Matthew inserts two little passages, somewhat reminiscent of folklore in character, to underline the point: Pilate's wife warns him of Jesus' innocence, and Pilate disclaims responsibility with a grand symbolic gesture. Nevertheless it remains absurd to justify anti-semitism by 'his blood be on us and on our children'; the numbers involved in the crowd were probably small, and it is doubtful whether they or even the high priests and elders could implicate the whole race in the guilt of their action. Even were this the case, anti-semitism would scarcely be the reaction Jesus himself would have recommended.

The scourging which normally followed sentence of death, forming indeed the preliminary part of the process of execution, could often result in death by itself. The *flagellum*, which the gospels indicate was used, was a form of whip used to execute prisoners by flogging.

How does Matthew wish his readers to see a Roman governor, the Jewish authorities, the crowd? To what extent are his views conditioned by the very different situation at the time he was writing?

Mt 27:27–31. Jesus crowned with thorns

Jesus was mocked by the Jews as a prophet, by the Romans as a king. The scarlet robe of a soldier obviously served to represent the emperor's purple toga. Here again the evangelist's interest is not in the pain but in the significance of the mockery, whose truth the soldiers cannot realise. Here also the prophecies of the suffering servant in Isaiah are fulfilled, as Jesus patiently bears their insults.

Mt 27:32–56. The crucifixion

The evangelists do not dwell on the details of the hideous process of crucifixion, which were all too familiar in the Roman world, for it was the normal means of execution of runaway slaves; nevertheless it was regarded by the not usually squeamish Romans as 'a most cruel and most frightful punishment'. The fixing of Jesus to the gibbet is passed over in a mere participle, with no mention of his sufferings. Instead they draw out the significance of the attendant circumstances.

Mark's account suggests that Simon of Cyrene was a christian (since his sons seem to be known to the community); in carrying the cross 'behind Jesus' (Luke) he is seen to be the model of christians. Many elements in this last scene are mentioned because even now Jesus is seen to be fulfilling details of the scriptures: Matthew calls the wine mixed with incense, which was usually given to prisoners as a narcotic, 'wine mixed with gall' because this corresponds to Ps 69 : 21; the division of his clothing and the mockery of Jesus as he hangs on the cross are described in such a way that their fulfilment of Ps 22 is made clear. It is this psalm which Jesus himself quotes from the cross, thus giving his own interpretation of his death. The gospels' use of scripture and treatment of the crucifixion suggests that Jesus' cry is not primarily one of dereliction, but must be understood precisely as the beginning of the psalm. In this prayer the psalmist describes his passage to a triumphant vindication through suffering and persecution; these therefore serve to bring all nations to acknowledge God, until finally (Ps 22 : 27) 'the whole earth, from end to end, will remember and come back to the Lord'. This, then, was the meaning of the crucifixion to the evangelists.

The contrast is marked between the conduct of Jew and gentile at the cross. The Jews taunt him, even challenging him to prove his claim to be son of God by saving himself from death. But it is the gentiles, the centurion and his company, who finally acknowledge him to be such. One of the soldiers undertakes the kindly gesture of offering him a drink, but is restrained by 'the rest of them' (? the Jews). The passing of salvation from the Jews to the gentiles is imminent and indeed takes place with the death of Jesus and the centurion's remark. Whether or not the centurion did intend his own words in the sense of acclaiming the divinity of Jesus, the evangelist certainly sees him as unwittingly professing it.

It is the cosmic disturbances which set the seal on the meaning of the crucifixion. They are the signs of God's awesome power intervening in the world, the terms in which his overwhelming support in battle or his withering punishment of the wicked were described in the old testament. So now the darkness and earthquake are accompanied by the rending of the veil of the temple to reveal the emptiness of the old rites, and by the rising of the dead from their tombs and the return of the faithful of Israel to the holy city—both signs of the arrival of the new age. How much the evangelist is giving a theological characterisation of the event of the crucifixion, or how much he is giving a material description of the phenomena which occurred is a matter of opinion. Even if these accompaniments of the crucifixion were not of the kind which could be observed, this would be the natural way for the evangelist to teach the significance of calvary.

Although Jesus had in mind the whole of psalm 22, yet the cry of dereliction stands out as particularly compelling

*and tragic. What weight can these words bear in the
light of our knowledge of Jesus as Son of God?*

Mt 27:57–66 (and 28:11–15). The burial

After a Roman execution the bodies were left to rot on
the gibbet, but to the Jews this would bring defilement
on the land, so Joseph goes to ask Pilate to bury the body.
But according to Jewish law bodies of criminals must
remain for a year in the public criminals' grave before
being returned to their families. We may therefore conclude that Joseph, 'a prominent member of the council'
(Mark) was the official charged with the public grave and
with the burial of criminals. But the evangelists are
anxious to mitigate as much as possible the shame of this
procedure: he was also a disciple of Jesus, the shroud was
clean and the tomb new (these last two epithets are inserted by Matthew; they are not in Mark's account, on
which he is drawing for the rest).   •

The burial of Jesus is an article of faith and an item
in the earliest preaching of the apostles because it is the
final proof of his humanity and of the reality of his death
—a source of hope also for us in the face of the seeming
hopelessness of burial. This is perhaps why the witness
of the Maries, who looked on, is mentioned.

Matthew's own passage on the guard at the tomb is
curious. It is full of features of Matthew's own style and
no other gospel mentions it. The first passage is a link,
preparing for the bribing of the guard by the high priests
in 28: 11–15. The excuse given to the guard there is so
transparently selfcontradictory that it is difficult to believe that it was invented by lawyers. However the story
certainly has a basis of truth: the public grave would
have a guard to prevent families from taking away the
bodies of their relatives, and no doubt the guards in-

vented some sort of lame excuse. But the little dialogues in each passage may well be elements of popular folklore which crept into Matthew's story, for neither has a ring of probability.

Is there any need for christians to prove 'scientifically' the truth of the gospels, or are we able to rely on the witness of faith?

Mt 28:1–10. The resurrection

The gospels contain no account of the resurrection itself. Was it indeed the sort of event which could be witnessed? In his glorified state Jesus was not at any rate permanently visible. The transformation which takes place at the resurrection of the body remains too mysterious for much to be said. For instance the gospels are agreed that Jesus was not immediately recognisable. Mark's and Matthew's accounts are not even centred on the fact of the empty tomb, for the women are not reported to have accepted the angel's invitation to enter it and see for themselves. The whole emphasis lies on the angel's message for the disciples, leading straight on to the climax of the gospel, Jesus' appearance in Galilee and the commission he there gives to the eleven. Luke, who has no appearances in Galilee, gives a different message, a short summary of the earliest preaching on the resurrection. Elsewhere in the scriptures a divine messenger or angel is used as a literary device for mediating the sense of an event intended by God. Here the accompanying phenomena suggest the same, only enough description being given to identify the apparition as a divine interpreter (the robe white as snow, the awestruck reaction of the woman); the earthquake here, as at the crucifixion, is a sign of the special presence and intervention of God. Are we then being faithful to the gospels if we understand Matthew to be saying, in a way intelligible to his contemporaries though foreign to us, that the women 'got the message' that Jesus was risen and that the disciples were to meet him in Galilee—a message for whose understanding guidance from God was required?

Why is the resurrection the greatest and most important event in Jesus' life, so that if there were no resurrection our faith would be in vain? (1 Cor 15:14)

Mt 28:16–20. Mission to the world

The details of the resurrection appearances of Christ differ so widely in Matthew, Luke and John (Mark mysteriously has none) that it is useless to attempt to reduce them to a single consecutive account. Matthew at any rate makes no attempt to give an account of the instruction which Christ gave to the disciples during the period in which he appeared to them before his final parting: instead he sums all up with this commission to preach to the world. It is as the glorious Lord, in the elevated and awesome solitude of the mountain, that he appears. The prophecy of Daniel of which he spoke before the high priest has been fulfilled, for 'all authority in heaven and on earth' has been given to him. And it is in this power that he sends out his messengers to all the world, and that he promises them his presence for ever, no mere passive being-with, but the active force of his power.

This conclusion is truly the climax of Matthew's gospel: Christ is seen clearly in the hieratic and all-embracing majesty which could be glimpsed in Matthew's portrait of Christ during his earthly life. But the climax is open-ended, for it establishes the conditions of the era of the church. During his earthly life Jesus' mission had been primarily to the Jews; with his death and resurrection the transition is made to the mission of the apostles to all nations. But it is still the mission of Christ, for his representatives are transfused with his presence and his power.

1. Is doubting a failure on man's part? (28 : 17)

2. What sense can we make of Jesus' statement concerning authority?

3. Do we christians realise that we are sharing in something which has cosmic significance? How does Christ's victory have such significance?

4. How can we best go forth and baptise in the name of the Father, Son and Holy Spirit?